*Accounting Irregularities
in Financial Statements*

違規會計

Accounting Irregularities in Financial Statements

違規會計

*A Definitive Guide for Litigators,
Auditors and Fraud Investigators*

BENNY K. B. KWOK

郭 啟 彬

GOWER

Published by
Gower Publishing Limited
Gower House
Croft Road
Aldershot
Hants GU11 3HR
England

Gower Publishing Company
Suite 420
101 Cherry Street
Burlington,
VT 05401-4405
USA

British Library Cataloguing in Publication Data
Kwok, Benny K.B.
  Accounting irregularities in financial statements: a
  definitive guide for litigators, auditors and fraud
  investigators
  1. Misleading financial statements 2. Accounting fraud
  3. Corporations - Accounting - Corrupt practices
  I. Title
  657.3

  ISBN 0 566 08621 2

Library of Congress Cataloging-in-Publication Data
Kwok, Benny K.B.
  Accounting irregularities in financial statements: a definitive guide for litigators,
  auditors and fraud investigators / by Benny K.B. Kwok.
    p. cm.
  ISBN: 0-566-08621-2
  1. Corporations--Accounting--Corrupt practices. 2. Financial statements. 3. Fraud.
4. Auditing, Internal. I. Title.
  HF5686.C7K85 2005
  657'.3--dc22

                                                          2005005509

Typeset by IML Typographers, Birkenhead, Merseyside.
Printed and bound in Great Britain by MPG Ltd, Bodmin.

3732513

Contents

List of Cases

List of Tables

List of Figures

Preface

Accounting Irregularities in Financial Statements is primarily designed for executives, litigators, auditors, accountants, investigators, legal counsels, law enforcement officers and other business professionals who have the responsibility of upholding the integrity of financial statements and deterring frauds and accounting irregularities. Regulators and standard-setters will find this book an excellent source of ideas and references when considering reforms and regulations. Educators and prospective accountants (including business and economics students) will see this book as an alternative, inspiring way of understanding accounting and how to stay alert to accounting irregularities in financial statements.

Capitalism and our modern society depend on trust: trust that governments are honouring their pledges; trust that citizens are fulfilling their obligations; trust that corporations are being diligently run; and trust that borrowers are paying their lenders. Most of these trusts hinge on properly prepared financial statements.

Accounting is not an exact science. Judgements must be exercised in many areas. In this sense, accounting is naturally creative, and changes are a constant feature. If you give a dozen accountants the same set of information and transactions about an organization and asked them to prepare a set of financial statements, it is likely that there would be variations and different results. What would change the phenomenon is the existence of a regulator who is often charged with the responsibility of reducing the variation of possible outcomes. The amount of the reduction would depend largely on the regulator's view of the role of judgement within the financial reporting environment.

This book is about accounting irregularities in financial statements. Accounting is a well-established subject, supported by a wide range of studies and literatures. Irregularities refer to accounting treatments and practices which are irregular and different from the acceptable standard, the generally accepted accounting principles (GAAP). Financial statements refer to the reports prepared by organizations in accounting for the results of the transactions and events in a defined time-frame.

There are two tiers of accounting irregularities. The first tier is to take advantage of the built-in flexibility of the GAAP. That means the irregularities may well fall within the accepted practices; but with a dishonest intent. Sometimes, the first tier is called 'creative accounting'. Strictly speaking, as long as the dishonest intent is proven, the perpetrators are still in breach because compliance with the GAAP also requires the correct selection and application of accounting practices within the GAAP. The selection and application processes also count in deciding whether or not an accounting irregularity has been committed.

The second tier refers to the attempts to breach the appropriate the GAAP and trying to hide the malpractices and irregularities. Once found, there would be no debate over the legitimacy of the malpractices and irregularities because, unlike the first tier, they are clearly in violation of GAAP (subject to court or disciplinary rulings).

This book uses the term 'organizations' to denote unincorporated businesses, commercial corporations, government authorities, quasi-government bodies and non-profit-making organizations because the distinctions amongst all these entities are not important as far as the contents of this book are concerned. What matters most is that the financial statements of all these organizations are bound by the GAAP, any departure from which are deemed to be accounting irregularities.

We have used the term 'auditor' to represent a range of parties, including investigators, tax assessors, forensic accountants and regulators. In many cases of accounting irregularites, officers in different institutions and authorities are asked to investigate the matters. They have their own scope and power to conduct the investigation. Going into the detail of the investigation will be beyond the scope of this book, thus we use one universal term to represent someone who is to investigate and report the findings of the accounting irregularities in question.

Cases in this book include fictitious names and any similarities are purely coincidental. Cases are adopted to illustrate the perpetration of accounting irregularities in financial statements. They only focus on particular aspects of a transaction(s) and are not a comprehensive discussion of all the relevant factors.

This book is organized so that readers who seek to learn about a particular topic do not have to read the entire book or preceding chapters to gain an understanding from the selected reading. However, the cost of presenting more self-contained chapters is some repetition. Readers of the entire book will note that some topics that have already been covered are briefly discussed a second (or third) time. While this is done to a very limited extent, it is done by design, allowing readers of selected chapters to gain the maximum from the time they invest in the book. This format may be helpful for the professional who has very high time costs.

Chapter 1 gives an overview of the financial reporting environments and the GAAP at the centre of it. Certain legislations, accounting standards and listing rules are discussed, and the concept of theft and false accounting are introduced. Chapter 2 describes the basics of accounting irregularities. Regardless of the exact form of the schemes, most perpetrators tend to rely on certain common areas in plotting the irregularities. Chapters 3 to 6 outline the tricks of accounting irregularities in four directions – 'selling more', 'costing less', 'owning more' and 'owing less'. In the context of GAAP, the chapters consider how perpetrators overstate revenues or assets and/or understate the expenses or liabilities of an organization. Chapter 7 considers various ways perpetrators may use to manipulate the classification and disclosure of financial statements. Chapter 8 illustrates three scenarios of accounting irregularities – tax evasion, theft and commercial dispute. Chapter 9 concludes this book by setting out various possible deterrents to accounting irregularities in two dimensions – micro and macro. At the micro-level, deterrents are implemented within the authority of the organization in question, while the macro-level deterrents refer to the external environment beyond the controls of any organization.

Acknowledgements

One does not author a book alone. I am indebted to every textbook and journal I have read and taught from, every seminar I have attended, every mentor I have learnt from, and every associate I have talked business with.

Special thanks go to the Institute of Chartered Accountants in England and Wales and the Hong Kong Institute of Certified Public Accountants that equipped me with the core qualifications upon which my professional career has been built.

Many people deserve thanks for the contributions they made to this book. Actions speak louder than words. I hope the success of *Accounting Irregularities in Financial Statements* will serve as a token of my appreciation towards all those who have helped or supported me during the writing and production of this book. True gratefulness from my heart – thank you.

BENNY K. B. KWOK
2005

CHAPTER 1

Overview of Financial Reporting Environments

Accounting, or more specifically financial reporting, is not a subject that can be gauged with complete precision. Financial reporting is not scientific and objective in the sense that science and engineering can be. No matter how intelligent and educated they might be, accountants cannot measure the financial performance of an organization in the same way that engineers can measure the weight of a piece of metal since there are not the same undisputed measurement criteria in accounting as there are in the case of engineering.

Accounting is founded on the basis of a business environment which, as we all know, is ever changing. Accounting is often known as the common language for business in translating the transactions and events into numbers and in communicating the financial performance to the outside world.

Financial statements are the summary of the accounting for a financial year prepared within an applicable financial reporting environment. There are no 'correct' financial statements as such. It is a balancing act between various factors on the basis of the availability of relevant records and the transactions and events that an organization might have undertaken.

From Chapters 3 to 8, we shall consider how accounting irregularities may exist in three main aspects of the financial statements which are:

- the profit and loss account (P&L)
- the balance sheet (B/S)
- notes to the financial statements (Notes).

There are other aspects (or components) of financial statements, such as cash flow statements, as governed by the jurisdiction to which an organization is subject. However, P&L, B/S and Notes are by far the dominant features attracting the most attention of readers of financial statements.

The term 'organization' is used throughout this book to include companies, partnerships, trusts, charities, sole proprietorship and other forms of entities requiring the preparation of financial statements in making economic decisions. In other words, financial reporting is driven by the information needs of the readers of financial statements. Typically, readers of financial statements include providers of finance, shareholders, employees, customers, vendors and governments.

The P&L is a statement in which revenues and expenditure are matched to arrive at a figure of profit or loss. Most organizations distinguish between a gross profit earned on trading and a net profit after other revenue and expenses. The P&L is arguably the most significant single indicator of an organization's success or failure. It is very important to ensure that it is not presented in such a way as to be misleading. This could happen either through an inconsistency within an organization or between different organizations; or it could arise as a result of deliberate manipulation of accounting figures.

The B/S is a statement of the assets, liabilities and capital of an organization at a given moment in time. It is like a 'snapshot' photograph, since it captures on paper a still image, frozen at a single moment in time, of something which is dynamic and continuously changing. Like any photograph, it can be taken from different angles and standpoints. The B/S gives an indication of what the business is worth at the end of the financial year, given a set of assumptions that are detailed in the Notes. The B/S is important to an organization because it is used to determine things such as the credit-worthiness, cost of funding and attractiveness to potential investors.

Notes are in narrative format and tend to be the largest part of the financial statements. They show the accounting policies used in the preparation of the financial statements and the basis of how all the numbers in the financial statements have been calculated. Understanding of the Notes is essential in detecting accounting irregularities.

GENERALLY ACCEPTED ACCOUNTING PRINCIPLES – GAAP

Generally accepted accounting principles (GAAP) is a term representing rules from all authoritative sources governing accounting. The primary sources of these rules are:

- statutory requirements of the jurisdiction to which the organization's financial statements are subject;
- accounting standards of the jurisdiction to which the organization's financial statements are subject;
- stock exchange requirements (for listed organizations).

In addition to the above sources, the basis of GAAP for individual jurisdictions may hinge on certain non-mandatory sources, such as:

- international accounting standards;

- statutory requirements in other jurisdictions (e.g. the influence from the US).

'Financial reporting environment' is a high-level umbrella term, covering a number of variables and components, such as GAAP, the frequency and distribution of financial statements, and the composition and function of the board of directors. Many of the key components of the financial reporting environment form an essential part of *corporate governance*. Corporate governance is a concept considered in Chapter 9 as a deterrent to accounting irregularities.

The ambit of the financial reporting environment can be drawn as a circle as shown in Figure 1.1. GAAP is at the centre, surrounded by other financial reporting rules and regulations, setting out the boundary in which the financial statements of organizations are being reported to their readers.

Figure 1.1   Circle of financial reporting environment and GAAP

In the US, the financial statements are required as 'fair presentation in accordance with GAAP' (which is equivalent to the 'true and fair view' in Hong Kong and the UK). GAAP are defined as those principles which have 'substantial authoritative support'. Therefore, financial statements prepared in accordance with accounting principles for which there is not substantial authoritative support are presumed to be misleading or inaccurate.

Although the term GAAP is widely used throughout this book, it is important to bear in mind that even as generally accepted, GAAP may not be relevant to all kinds of organizations in all circumstances. Any accounting practice which is appropriate in a particular circumstance should be regarded as GAAP. Whether or not such a practice has been generally adopted or commonly used is not necessarily the overriding consideration. In addition, the term 'generally accepted' in GAAP implies a high degree of practical application of a particular accounting practice. However, there are newly introduced GAAP and new areas of accounting which have not, as yet, been generally applied. There are frequently different accounting treatments for similar items, and they are all generally accepted.

The general views shared in Hong Kong and the UK are that, as evidenced by the constantly changing legislations, accounting standards and stock exchange listing requirements, GAAP is a dynamic concept constantly being reviewed and adapted in response to changing business priorities and economic environments. As circumstances change, different accounting practices are adopted accordingly. GAAP goes far beyond rigid rules and principles, and anticipates emerging contemporary accounting practices. A conceptual framework is established by the accounting profession in Hong Kong and the UK[1] as well as the US. Applying a conceptual framework in financial reporting is an attempt to codify and test the consistency of existing GAAP and to assist the development of future standards.[2]

FINANCIAL REPORTING ENVIRONMENT IN HONG KONG

In Hong Kong, the financial reporting environment is based on three principal sources:

- Companies Ordinance – Chapter 32

- Accounting standards, or more specifically the Statements of Standard Accounting Practices (SSAP) – all SSAP are being changed and renamed as the Hong Kong Accounting Standards (HKAS), which themselves are to be phased out gradually and replaced by the Hong Kong Financial Reporting Statements (HKFRS) as from 1 January 2005

- Listing rules.

Hong Kong, a British colony until 1997, has a common law jurisdiction. An outline of the financial reporting requirements is set out in the Companies Ordinance. Accounting rules and more specific details are developed by the self-regulated private sector through accounting standards and listing rules.

COMPANIES ORDINANCE

In Hong Kong, companies incorporated under the Companies Ordinance are required to maintain proper books of account, so as to show at any time a true and fair view of the state of the company's affairs and to explain its transactions.[3]

Such books must include details of receipts and payments, sales and purchases of goods, and the assets and liabilities of the company.[4] The books of account must be kept at the registered office of the company or at another location chosen by the directors, provided that, if the books are kept outside Hong Kong, sufficient information is maintained in Hong Kong to disclose with reasonable accuracy the financial position of the company at any time.[5] The books of account must also be kept for seven years from the end of the financial year to which they relate.[6]

Every company registered under the Companies Ordinance is also required to prepare:

- a B/S which gives a true and fair view of the state of affairs of the company as at the end of its financial year; and

- a P&L which gives a true and fair view of the profit or loss of the company for the financial year.[7]

The requirement for a true and fair view overrides all other accounting requirements of the Companies Ordinance, accounting standards or listing rules. For example, if the financial statements drawn up in compliance with the detailed requirements of the Companies Ordinance do not give sufficient information to present a true and fair view, then the necessary additional information should be given in the financial statements.

The financial statements must be approved by the board of directors and signed on their behalf by two directors on the face of the B/S.[8] A copy of the financial statements, together with the auditors' report and directors' report on those financial statements, must be sent to every member and debenture holder not less than 21 days before the date of the annual general meeting.[9] The audited financial statements of a company must be presented to the shareholders of the company at the annual general meeting and the financial statements should be made up to a date falling not more than six months before the date of the annual general meeting.[10] The directors of a company, other than a private company, must include a copy of the audited annual financial statements, auditors' report and directors' report in the company's annual return to the Registrar of Companies within 42 days following the annual general meeting.[11]

While the main body of the Companies Ordinance dictates when and which companies must prepare financial statements, the Tenth Schedule is primarily concerned with the specific disclosure requirements in their financial statements. The financial reporting information required by the Tenth Schedule includes:

- the basis on which the amount of Hong Kong profits tax is calculated;

- the basis on which turnover for the year is arrived at;

- details on finance costs;

- auditors' remuneration;

- details of land leases held;

- details on other investments, distinguishing between listed and unlisted portions, and related outstanding indebtedness;

- details on capital commitments, whether authorized or contracted for;

- aggregate amount of loans to trustees or employees; and

- details on debentures, loans and bank overdrafts, including details of secured liabilities.

ACCOUNTING STANDARDS

The Hong Kong Institute of Certified Public Accountants (HKICPA) (previously known as the Hong Kong Society of Accountants until September 2004) is the only statutory body (constituted under the Professional Accountants Ordinance) to license and regulate professional accountants in Hong Kong. The HKICPA may, in relation to the practice of accountancy, issue or specify any standards of accounting practices required to be observed, maintained or otherwise applied by its members.

The HKICPA has been developing accounting standards to achieve convergence with the International Financial Reporting Standards (IFRS) issued by the International Accounting Standards Board (IASB). The HKICPA develops and publishes HKAS and HKFRS and promotes the use of those standards in general purpose financial statements and other financial reporting. Other financial reporting comprises information provided outside financial statements, which assists in the interpretation of a complete set of financial statements or improves readers' ability to make efficient economic decisions.

Statements of Standard Accounting Practice (SSAP) cover recognition, measurement and disclosure issues on a wide range of topics. SSAP (and the emerging HKAS and HKFRS) are the most authoritative source of GAAP in Hong Kong. Although they do not have any statutory backing, their authority is ensured by the HKICPA's requirement that they be observed by its members involved (either as preparers or as auditors) with financial statements intended to give a true and fair view (that is, the overriding requirements as set out in the Companies Ordinance), unless there are justifiable reasons for a departure in very exceptional circumstances.

In 1998, the HKICPA formed an Urgent Issues and Interpretations Sub-Committee (UIISC). The principal task of the UIISC is to develop interpretations on the application of SSAP on a timely basis in areas that have, or are considered likely to receive, divergent or unacceptable treatment.

Interpretations are authoritative guidance on the application of SSAP and have the same status as the background material and implementation guidance contained in SSAP.[12]

Accounting Guidelines (AG) have effect as guidance statements and indicators of best practice.[13] They are persuasive in intent. Unlike SSAP, AG are not mandatory, but are consistent with the purpose of SSAP in that they help define accounting practice in the particular area or sector to which they refer. Therefore, they should normally be followed, and members of the HKICPA should be prepared to explain departures if called upon to do so. Many AG issued previously have already been superseded by the publication of a new accounting standard which addresses and sets out mandatory practice in relation to accounting issues which were previously the subject of an AG.

The *Framework for the Preparation and Presentation of Financial Statements* (Framework), issued by the HKICPA, sets out the concepts underlying the preparation and presentation of financial statements for external readers and provides guidance for dealing with issues that are not covered by extant SSAP or AG.

Even though the application of the Framework is not mandatory, financial statements which are inconsistent with it, without the support of an applicable SSAP or AG, may still be deemed as irregular.

Accounting Bulletins (AB) are informative publications on subjects of topical interest and are intended to assist members of the HKICPA or to stimulate debate on important accounting issues.[14] They do not have the same authority as either accounting standards or AG.

With effect from 1 January 2005, all the existing SSAP and SSAP Interpretations for which there are equivalent International Accounting Standards (IAS) and IAS Interpretations will be renamed as Hong Kong Accounting Standards (HKAS) and HKAS Interpretations with numbers corresponding to the equivalent IAS and IAS Interpretations, respectively.

LISTING RULES

As their shares are in the hands of the general public, listed companies need to disclose more information in their financial statements. The rules governing the Listing of Securities of the Stock Exchange of Hong Kong (SEHK) are referred as the listing rules.

Companies listed in Hong Kong may be incorporated in Hong Kong or overseas, which are subject to different jurisdictions. Companies listed on the Main Board of the SEHK are required to send their annual reports and audited financial statements to every member and other holders of their securities within four months after the financial year-end, and not less than 21 days before the date of the annual general meeting.

The listing rules require certain financial information disclosures, other than those required by the Companies Ordinance or the accounting standards, which are normally presented in the Notes. These disclosures include:

- analysis of the maturity profile of borrowings;
- analysis of directors' emoluments by emolument band;
- analysis of employees' emoluments by emolument band;
- pension schemes;
- credit policy and aged analysis of accounts receivable; and
- aged analysis of accounts payable.

Listed companies are also required to publish in the newspapers a preliminary announcement of final results the next business day after they are authorized for issue by the board of directors. Details of the results should also be made available on the SEHK's official website for public inspection.

A listed company is required to issue an interim report for the first six months of a financial year. This report must be published not later than three months after the end of that interim period.

The main requirements of the Listing Rules for the basis of preparation of financial statements by companies listed in Hong Kong on the Main Board are set out as follows:

- All companies with a primary listing, or in the process of obtaining a primary listing on the Main Board, are allowed to prepare financial statements in accordance with the GAAP in Hong Kong or IAS. Companies adopting IAS are required to explain and compile a statement of the financial effect of material differences between the financial statements presented under IAS and those that would have been presented under Hong Kong GAAP. However, this requirement for reconciliation to Hong Kong GAAP does not apply to the companies incorporated in Mainland China (Hong Kong is a Special Administrative Region of the People's Republic of China).

- Overseas companies with a secondary listing on the Main Board are permitted to use the GAAP in the US.

Other than the Main Board, the second tier of the SEHK is known as the Growth Enterprises Market.

FINANCIAL REPORTING ENVIRONMENT IN THE UK

In the UK, the financial reporting environment is based on three principal sources:

- Companies Act 1985 and the Companies Act 1989

- Accounting standards, or more specifically the Statements of Standard Accounting Practices (SSAP) and the Financial Reporting Standards (FRS)

- the listing requirements of the Stock Exchange ('Yellow Book').

As in Hong Kong, the financial reporting environment is outlined by statute, supplemented by the self-regulated private sector through accounting standards and listing rules.

COMPANIES ACT

The Companies Act 1985 consolidated the bulk of previous company legislations. This was substantially amended by the Companies Act 1989. Since the UK became a member of the European Union (EU), it has been obliged to comply with the legal requirements of the EU. It does this by enacting UK laws to implement EU directives, such as the provisions of the seventh and eighth EU directives, which deal with consolidated financial statements and auditors.

Accounting records maintained by every company must:[15]

- be sufficient to show and explain the company's transactions;

- disclose with reasonable accuracy at any time the financial position of the company at that time; and

- enable the directors to ensure that any P&L or B/S gives a true and fair view of the company's financial position.

Accounting records should contain:[16]

- day-to-day entries for money received and paid, with an explanation of why the receipts and payments occurred (the nature of the transactions);

- a record of the company's assets and liabilities; and

- where the company deals in goods:
  - statements of stocks held at the financial year-end;
  - statements of stock takings on which the figures in the statements of stocks are based; and
  - with the exception of goods sold on retail, statements of all goods bought and sold identifying for each items the suppliers or customers.

Under section 145(B) of the Companies Act 1985, where the financial statements of a company do not comply with the requirements of the Act, the court may order the preparation of revised financial statements, and that all or part of the costs be borne by such of the directors as were party to the approval of the defective financial statements. Accounting records are to be kept at the registered office of the company or at such other place as the directors think fit, and they should be open to inspection at all times by officers of the company.[17]

Every company must keep official records and these are usually delegated to the company secretary. They include registers of:

- present and past directors and company secretaries;

- directors' interests in the company's shares and debentures;

- shareholders past and present and their shareholdings;

- any charges on the company's assets – where the assets are used as security for borrowing;

- debenture holders – usually banks.

Companies are also required to preserve their accounting records for three years in respect of private companies or for six years for other companies. A company is considered to be private unless it is registered as a public company.

In the UK, every limited company is required to produce financial statements which show a true and fair view of the company's results for the financial year and its financial position at the end of the financial year. The B/S shall give a true and fair view of the state of affairs of the company as at the end of the financial year, and the P&L shall give a true and fair view of the profit or loss of the company for the financial year.[18]

Neither the Companies Acts nor the accounting standards define the term 'true and fair view'. As the accounting standards are subject to a continuous reviewing process, a question arises as to whether the concept defined by 'true and fair view' is constant or is changeable over a period of years.

Although the statute lays down numerous rules on the information to be included in the published financial statements and the format of its presentation, any such rule may be overridden if compliance with it would prevent the financial statements from showing a true and fair view.[19] Therefore, the requirement that the financial statements show a true and fair view is paramount. If a B/S or P&L drawn up in compliance with these other requirements of the Act would not provide enough information to give a true and fair view, then any necessary additional information must also be given.

The overriding priority to give a true and fair view has in the past been treated as an important loophole in the law, and has caused some debates within the accounting profession. If companies do depart from the other requirements of the Act in order to give a true and fair view, they must explain the particulars of and reasons for the departure, and its effects on the financial statements, in the Notes.

A directors' report must be prepared and attached to the B/S.[20] The signature of one director on the B/S is evidence of the approval of the accounts by the board. Once this has been done, and the auditors have completed their report, the accounts are laid before the members of the company in the general meeting.

The directors shall lay before the company in general meeting and also deliver to the Registrar, in respect of each financial year-end, a copy of every document comprising the financial statements for that financial year.[21] However, the Companies Act 1989 has subsequently amended this provision to allow the members of private companies to elect unanimously to dispense with general meeting. This does not, however, exempt the company from providing financial statements to members. The period allowed for laying before and delivering financial statements is ten months after the end of the financial year for private companies,[22] or seven months for other public companies.

Once prepared, a copy of the accounts, auditors' report and directors' report must be sent to the Registrar of Companies, who maintains a separate file for every company. The Registrar's files may be inspected for a nominal fee by any member of the public. This is why the statutory accounts are often referred to as published financial statements. Unlimited companies (with some exceptions) are exempt from the duty to deliver copies of their financial statements to the Registrar of Companies.

The B/S and P&L should also comply with the requirements of the Fourth

Schedule,[23] and there are two formats for the B/S (horizontal and vertical) and two horizontal and two vertical formats for the P&L. Once a company has chosen a format it must adhere to it for subsequent financial years unless, in the opinion of the directors, there are special reasons for a change. Details of any change and the reason for it must be disclosed in the Notes.

Copies of the financial statements must be sent to every shareholder at least 21 days before any general meeting at which the financial statements will be presented, and the shareholders are allowed to inspect the minutes of a general meeting and to have a copy of them.

ACCOUNTING STANDARDS

Similar to Hong Kong, all accounting standards in the UK used to be called Statements of Standard Accounting Practice (SSAP) and were until 31 July 1990 formulated by the Accounting Standard Committee (ASC). SSAP are gradually being replaced by Financial Reporting Standards (FRS) produced by the successor to the ASC, the Accounting Standards Board (ASB). The SSAP which were in force at the date the ASB was formed have been adopted by the ASB. They are gradually being superseded by the new FRS.

Accounting standards are applicable to financial statements of an organization that are intended to give a true and fair view of its state of affairs at the B/S date and of its P&L for the financial year-ending on that date. Accounting standards need not be applied to immaterial items. Where accounting standards are authoritative, statements of how particular types of transactions and other events should be reflected in financial statements, and accordingly compliance with accounting standards will normally be necessary for financial statements to give a true and fair view. In applying accounting standards, it is important to be guided by the spirit and reasoning behind them.

An exposure draft is issued for comment and is subject to revision. Until it is converted into an accounting standard, the requirements of any existing accounting standards that would be affected by proposals in the exposure draft remain in force.

The *Statement of Principles for Financial Reporting* issued by the ASB sets out the principles that the ASB believes should underlie the preparation and presentation of company financial statements. This is not itself an accounting standard, and its primary purpose is to assist the ASB in the development and review of accounting standards and to provide those interested in its work with an understanding of the ASB's approach to the formulation of accounting standards.

The ASB has published its Statement of Aims which set out the ASB's general approach to its task and lists a number of fundamental guidelines which it follows in conducting its affairs. In addition to issuing exposure drafts of FRS and of Statement of Aims, the ASB also publishes discussion papers on individual topics as they reach appropriate stages of development.

THE STOCK EXCHANGE LISTING REQUIREMENTS – YELLOW BOOK

As their shares are in the hands of the general public, listed companies need to disclose more information in their financial statements. The rules governing the listing of securities of the Stock Exchange in the UK are referred to as the Yellow Book. Listed companies are expected to issue their financial statements within six months of their financial year-end, although they may apply for an extension if they have significant overseas interests. However, most listed companies will report within three months of their financial year-end.

In addition to those required by the Companies Act 1985 and 1989 and the accounting standards, the Yellow Book requires certain financial information disclosure and is normally presented in the Notes. These disclosures include:

- details of loans, overdrafts and other borrowings;

- amount of interest capitalized;

- whether or not the company is a close company;

- details of significant contracts in which any director is materially interested and for the provision of services by any shareholder with 30 per cent or more of the voting power;

- details of the waiving of any emoluments by a director; the identity of each independent non-executive director together with their brief biographical details; details of each director's beneficial and non-beneficial interests in the company's shares and options;

- the reason for the difference between the actual results and the published profit forecast (if such difference is over 10 per cent);

- the principal country in which each subsidiary operates and details of each associate undertaking;

- any departure from UK or other accounting standards as applicable to the company and the reasons for non-compliance;

- the combined code on corporate governance – this applies only to companies incorporated in the UK together with a review by the auditors and any reasons for non-compliance;

- details of the waiving of any dividends by a shareholder; information on shareholdings of 3 per cent or more of any class of voting shares, that are not owned by the directors; details of any authority for the purchase by the company of its own shares, and details of any purchases that were not made through the market; details of shares that were issued for cash, unless this issue was in the form of a rights issue; if the company has listed shares in issue and is the subsidiary of another company, it must disclose the parent's participation in any placing of its shares.

INTERNATIONAL PERSPECTIVE

Like Hong Kong and the UK, most well-developed jurisdictions have their own regulatory framework for financial reporting and the preparation of financial statements. However, there is also an international arena which is becoming more important as the financial markets become more globalized and require more comparable information amongst organizations. International financial reporting framework first started in 1973 with the creation of the International Accounting Standards Committee which was an independent private sector body and had no formal authority. Many jurisdictions adopted international accounting standards (IAS) to avoid developing their own, or changed IAS to tailor to their circumstances.

The IAS were flexible and in many cases allowed alternative treatments. In 1995, the IASC entered into an agreement with the International Organization of Securities Commissions (IOSCO) and had completed a core set of standards. These core standards were endorsed by the IOSCO as an appropriate reporting regime for business entities in the global marketplace for the raising of finance, that is, the stock exchanges worldwide. This gave the IASC the authority, and in 2000 the IASC was restructured and became the International Accounting Standards Board (IASB). The core standards were accepted by the IOSCO in 2000.

The IASB is governed by a group of 19 individual trustees with diverse geographical and functional backgrounds. The trustees form the IASC Foundation and they are responsible for governance, fund-raising and public awareness of the IASB. The IASB is solely responsible for setting International Finance Reporting Standards and has 12 full-time members and two part-time. The current structure also includes a Standards Interpretation Committee and a Standards Advisory Council, both of which sit alongside the IASB.

THEFT AND FALSE ACCOUNTING

THEFT

In Hong Kong, theft is defined in the Theft Ordinance 1970. In the UK, theft is defined in the Theft Act 1968.

It is provided that a person is guilty of theft if they dishonestly appropriate property belonging to another with the intention of permanently depriving the other of it; and 'thief' and 'steal' shall be construed accordingly.[24] It is immaterial whether the appropriation is made with a view to gaining, or is made for the thief's own benefit.[25]

Theft is an offence, and punishable on conviction or indictment by imprisonment for a term not exceeding ten years. A person who by any deception dishonestly obtains property belonging to another with the intention of permanently depriving the other of it commits an offence.[26] Obtaining property covers obtaining or retaining ownership, possession or control of it. Deception means any deception, deliberate or reckless, by words or conduct as to fact or law, including a deception as to the present intention of the person using the deception or any other person. A person who by any deception dishonestly obtains for himself or another any pecuniary advantage commits an offence.[27]

The Theft (Amendment) Ordinance 1980 of Hong Kong and the Theft Act 1978 of the UK create a range of offences as follows:

- dishonestly obtaining services from another by deception;
- evading liability by deception (the offence is committed where a person by deception dishonestly secures the remission of a liability to make payment, or, with intent to make permanent default, dishonestly induces a creditor or person claiming payment on their behalf to wait for or forgo payment, or dishonestly obtains exemption from or abatement of liability to make payment);
- dishonestly making off without payment, where it is known that payment on the spot is required or expected, and with intent to avoid payment.

FALSE ACCOUNTING

A person who makes or concurs in making an entry which is or may be misleading, false or deceptive in a material particular, or who omits or concurs in omitting a material particular, is treated as falsifying the account or document. False accounting refers to an offence:[28]

- to dishonestly destroy, deface, conceal or falsify any account or record or document made or required for any accounting purpose; or

- in furnishing information for any purpose dishonestly to produce or make use of any account or any record or document as aforesaid which, to the knowledge of the person producing or making use of it, is or may be misleading, false or deceptive in a material particular, with a view to gaining for oneself or another or with intent to causing loss to another.

Gain includes a gain (temporary or permanent) by keeping what one has, as well as a gain by getting what one has not, and loss includes a loss by not getting what one might get, as well as a loss by parting with what one has.[29]

OTHER OFFENCES

Where the officer of a company or an unincorporated entity, with intent to deceive members or creditors about its affairs, publishes or concurs in publishing a written statement or account which to the knowledge of the officer is or may be misleading, false or deceptive in a material particular, the officer commits an offence (that is, false statements by directors).[30]

A person who dishonestly, with a view to gaining for themselves (or another) or with intent to causing loss to another, destroys, defaces or conceals any valuable security (any will or other testamentary document or any original document of, or belonging to, or filed or deposited in, any court or any government department) commits an offence (that is, suppression of documents).[31] Similarly, a person who dishonestly procures execution of a valuable security commits an offence. This applies in relation to the making, acceptance, endorsement, alteration, cancellation or destruction in whole or in part of a valuable security, and in relation to the signing or sealing of any paper or other material in order that it may be made or converted into, or used or dealt with as a valuable security, as if that were the execution of a valuable security. A valuable security means any document creating, transferring, surrendering or releasing any right to, in or over property, or authorizing the payment of money or delivery of any property, or evidencing the creation, transfer, surrender or release of any such right, or the payment of money or delivery of any property, or the satisfaction of any obligation.

CONCLUSION

This chapter attempts to provide a brief outline of the financial reporting environment in Hong Kong and the UK. To obtain a detailed understanding of this comprehensive topic, a review of a wide range of literatures and legislations will be required which is beyond the scope of this book.

An awareness of the financial reporting environment is vital in understanding accounting irregularities in financial statements. The financial reporting environment in Hong Kong and the UK are very similar, and may be largely viewed in terms of three layers. The first and basic layer is the laws, upon which the accounting standards are established in setting out more detailed rules and may be seen as the second layer. The third and top layer includes the listing rules, recommendations and best practices.

Accounting irregularities are normally a means to an end rather than an end by itself. One possible motive underneath some accounting irregularities may well be to fabricate a situation allowing the misappropriation of assets, theft, to take place. Both in Hong Kong and the UK, the laws have set out clearly the meaning of theft and the possible penalties on convicted thieves.

Notes

1, 2 – The HKICPA, *Framework for the Preparation and Presentation of Financial Statements*
(issued in June 1997 and revised in May 2003)
– The ASB, *Statement of Principles for Financial Reporting* (issued in December 1999)
3 – The Companies Ordinance, Hong Kong, section 121(2)
4 – The Companies Ordinance, Hong Kong, section 121(1)
5 – The Companies Ordinance, Hong Kong, section 121(3)
6 – The Companies Ordinance, Hong Kong, section 121(3A)
7 – The Companies Ordinance, Hong Kong, section 123
8 – The Companies Ordinance, Hong Kong, section 129B(1)
9 – The Companies Ordinance, Hong Kong, section 129G
10 – The Companies Ordinance, Hong Kong, section 122
11 – The Companies Ordinance, Hong Kong, section 109
12, 13, 14 – The HKICPA, *Preface to Hong Kong Financial Reporting Standards* (issued in October
2003)
15, 16 – The Companies Act 1985, UK, section 221
17 – The Companies Act 1985, UK, section 222
18 – The Companies Act 1985, UK, section 226
19 – The Companies Act 1985, UK, section 226(5)
20 – The Companies Act 1985, UK, section 234
21 – The Companies Act 1985, UK, section 241
22 – The Companies Act 1985, UK, section 244
23 – The Companies Act 1985, UK, section 226(3)
24, 25 – The Theft Ordinance, Hong Kong
– The Theft Act 1968, UK
26 – The Theft Ordinance, Hong Kong, section 17
– The Theft Act 1968, UK, section 15
27 – The Theft Ordinance, Hong Kong, section 18
– The Theft Act 1968, UK, section 16
28 – The Theft Ordinance, Hong Kong, section 19
– The Theft Act 1968, UK, section 17
29 – The Theft Ordinance, Hong Kong, section 8(2)
– The Theft Act 1968, UK, section 34(3)
30 – The Theft Ordinance, Hong Kong, section 21
– The Theft Act 1968, UK, section 19
31 – The Theft Ordinance, Hong Kong, section 22
– The Theft Act 1968, UK, section 20

CHAPTER 2

Basics of Accounting Irregularities

PURPOSES OF ACCOUNTING

The meaning and ambit of generally accepted accounting principles have been considered in Chapter 1. Any accounting practices which are in violation of generally accepted accounting principles (GAAP) are deemed to be irregular. In other words, accounting irregularities contradict the objective of accounting and defeat the spirit of having GAAP in place.

In this chapter, we shall consider three critical questions:

- What are the purposes of accounting?
- How do accounting irregularities try to overturn these objectives?
- What are the basics of accounting irregularities adopted by most perpetrators?

The traditional purposes of accounting are to classify and record monetary transactions and to present the financial result of an organization. It is traditionally known as 'stewardship', and investors are assumed to have delegated the responsibility of the day-to-day running of the business to the management who then use the financial statements to present information to the owners or investors showing how their funds have been utilized, and what profits have derived from such use.

These traditions have since evolved, and accounting now exists in a much broader context. In order to reflect the changing community expectations about the performance and responsibilities of business, some academics even argue that accounting should serve as a mechanism in reporting an organization's social and environmental performance. Rather than a comprehensive academic text in accounting, this book is primarily concerned with accounting irregularities in financial statements. In this chapter and for the rest of this book, we follow the mainstream thoughts and practices in accounting.

In Hong Kong, the HKICPA issued the *Framework for the Preparation and Presentation of Financial Statements* (Framework) in June 1997 (revised May 2003).

According to the Framework, the objective of financial statements is to provide information about the financial position, performance and changes in financial position of an organization that is useful to a wide range of readers (or users) in making economic decisions. Financial statements also show the results of the stewardship of management, or the accountability of management for the resources entrusted to it.

In the UK, the ASB issued *Statement of Principles for Financial Reporting* (Principle) in December 1999. According to the Principle, the objective of financial statements is to provide information about an organization's financial performance and financial position that is useful to a wide range of readers for assessing the stewardship of the organization's management and for making economic decisions. That objective can usually be met by focusing exclusively on the information needs of present and potential investors.

In fact, the Framework does not differ significantly from the Principle; both are consistent with the *Framework for the Preparation and Presentation of Financial Statements* issued by the International Accounting Standards Committee.

It is not difficult to identify the readers of financial statements or their requirements for information. The difficulties arise only from what is primarily a subjective judgement as to which readers are entitled to what kinds of information.[1] Unfortunately, there exists little agreement on what kinds of information are considered essential in such areas. Readers of financial statements can be defined along a spectrum of those having reasonable rights to information of the organization as shown in Figure 2.1.[2] However, there is no consensus as to who is entitled to have access to what is often classified as commercially sensitive information, and who is not.

Investors   General public

Figure 2.1   Spectrum of readers of financial statements

At one end of the spectrum, investors are seen to have the most direct interest because it is their money which is at stake if the organization goes under.[3] This is in line with the stewardship concept which requires highly verifiable data to be presented because all parties in question demand reasonable certainty of the facts, especially in a legal dispute.

At the other end of the spectrum, the widest definition of readers is the general public.[4] Although there is no direct, contractual relationship between the organization and the public, other than in their capacities as investors or other specific groups (such as employees, customers and suppliers), the public's right to information arises from the role played in our society by these organizations. They compete for resources of manpower, materials and energy, make use of community infrastructures, and affect the environment. For example, the call for environmental accounting and auditing is a direct result of the rising concerns over the commercial organizations' exploitation of the natural environment for their own benefits.

ACCOUNTING IRREGULARITIES

Accounting irregularities are not formally defined in the GAAP. Reference may be made to the auditing standards which set out the requirements for auditors to follow in the audits of financial statements.

In Hong Kong, the HKICPA issued the Statement of Auditing Standards (SAS) 110 *The Auditors' Responsibility to Consider Fraud and Error in an Audit of Financial Statements* in February 2002, effective for audits of financial statements for periods ending on or after 31 March 2002. In the UK, Statements of Auditing Standards (SAS) 110 *Fraud and Error* was issued by the Auditing Practice Board (APB) in January 1995, effective for audits of financial statements for accounting periods ending on or after 30 June 1995.

Mis-statements in financial statements, that is accounting irregularities, can arise from error or fraud. Error refers to an unintentional mis-statement in financial statements, including the omission of an amount or a disclosure, such as:[5]

- a mistake in gathering or processing data from which financial statements are prepared;

- an incorrect accounting estimate arising from oversight or misinterpretation of facts; and

- a mistake in the application of accounting principles relating to measurement, recognition, classification, presentation, or disclosure.

Fraud comprises both the use of deception to obtain an unjust or illegal financial advantage and intentional misrepresentations affecting the financial statements by one or more individuals among management, employees or third parties. Fraud may involve:[6]

- falsification or alteration of accounting records or other documents;

- misappropriation of assets or theft;

- suppression or omission of the effects of transactions from records or documents;

- recording of transactions without substance;

- intentional misapplication of accounting policies; or

- wilful misrepresentations of transactions or of the organization's state of affairs.

Although fraud is a broad legal concept, the auditors are concerned with fraudulent acts that cause a material mis-statement in the financial statements. Mis-statement of the financial statements may not be the objective of some frauds. Fraud involving one or more members of management or those charged with governance is referred to as 'management fraud'; fraud involving only employees of the entity is referred to as 'employee fraud'. In either case, there may be collusion with third parties outside the organization.

Two types of intentional mis-statements are relevant to the auditors' consideration of fraud[7] – mis-statements resulting from fraudulent financial reporting and mis-statements resulting from misappropriation of assets.

Fraudulent financial reporting, which is a main type of accounting irregularity, involves intentional mis-statements or omissions of amounts or disclosures in financial statements to deceive the readers of financial statements. Fraudulent financial reporting may involve:

- deception such as manipulation, falsification, or alteration of accounting records or supporting documents from which the financial statements are prepared;

- misrepresentation in, or intentional omission from, the financial statements of events, transactions or other significant information; and

- intentional misapplication of accounting principles relating to measurement, recognition, classification, presentation or disclosure.

Misappropriation of assets involves the theft of an organization's assets. Misappropriation of assets can be accomplished in a variety of ways (including embezzling receipts, stealing physical or intangible assets, or causing an organization to pay for goods and services not received). Misappropriation of assets is often accompanied by false or misleading records or documents in order to conceal the fact that the assets are missing, indirectly causing accounting irregularities in financial statements.

The difference between fraud and error is whether the underlying action that results in the mis-statement in the financial statements is intentional or unintentional. Unlike error, fraud is intentional and usually involves deliberate concealment of the facts. While the auditors may be able to identify potential opportunities for fraud to be perpetrated, it is difficult, if not impossible, for the auditors to determine intent, particularly in matters involving management judgement, such as accounting estimates and the appropriate application of accounting principles.

Compliance with either of the two SAS 110 (HKICPA and APB) ensures compliance in all material respects with the basic principles and essential procedures in International Standard on Auditing (ISA) 240 *The Auditor's Responsibility to Consider Fraud and Error in an Audit of Financial Statements.*

The preparation of financial statements call for expertise and experience in financial reporting as well as the skilful application of these in the real commercial world. All these are based on certain fundamental accounting concepts and the double-entry book-keeping process within the financial reporting environment. The financial reporting environment in Hong Kong and the UK has been discussed in Chapter 1. A good understanding of the basics of accounting irregularities can be achieved by examining certain fundamental concepts of financial accounting, the key components of double-entry book-keeping and how all these relate and interact.

Let us consider all these in the subsequent three sections:

● Accounting policies in financial statements

● Fundamental concepts in financial reporting

● Double-entry book-keeping and accounting equation.

ACCOUNTING POLICIES IN FINANCIAL STATEMENTS

In Hong Kong, the HKICPA issued SSAP 1 *Presentation of Financial Statements* in March 1984 (revised May 1999, August 2001 and December 2001), effective for accounting periods starting on or after 1 January 2002. In order to ensure comparability both with the organization's own financial statements of previous financial years and with the financial statements of other organizations, SSAP 1 of the HKICPA sets out overall considerations for the presentation of financial statements, guidelines for their structure and minimum requirements for the content of financial statements.

In the UK, the ASB issued FRS 18 *Accounting Policies* in December 2000, effective for accounting periods ending on or after 22 June 2001. FRS 18 sets out the principles to be followed in selecting accounting policies and the disclosures for the readers to understand the accounting policies adopted and how they have been applied. It requires specific disclosures about the adopted accounting policies and changes to those policies and, in some circumstances, disclosures about the estimation techniques used in applying those policies.

Accounting policies are the principles, bases, conventions, rules and practices adopted by an organization in preparing and presenting financial statements.[8] In essence, accounting policies specify how the effects of transactions and other events are to be reflected in financial statements through recognizing, measuring and presenting assets, liabilities, gains, losses and changes to capital (or shareholders' funds).[9]

Observing SSAP 1 of the HKICPA and FRS 18 of the ASB ensures compliance in all material respects with International Accounting Standard IAS 1 (revised 1997) *Presentation of Financial Statements.*

At present, an organization has a great deal of flexibility to choose amongst alternative ways of presenting its financial performance and position. It is not only about selecting an attractive layout but also including choices that determine within legitimate limits of how an organization's results and financial position would look.[10] Two identical organizations with the same value and volume of purchases and sales may produce two rather different profit figures simply due to differences in accounting policies or estimation techniques. Examples include different methods of depreciation (straight-line and reducing-balance), different methods used to estimate the proportion of doubtful debts and different stock valuation policies (first-in-first-out and average cost).[11] However, it is important to bear in mind that, over a long period of time, there is little that accounting can do to alter the cumulative profit,[12] except occasionally by influencing the amount of taxation (see Figure 2.2 in the subsequent section), as long as the financial statements are in full compliance with the GAAP.

Exercising an excessive degree of selectivity along the edge or outside the boundary of the GAAP is often known as 'creative accounting' and may be regarded as generating accounting irregularities in financial statements. Creative accounting can be looked at in two tiers: creativity within the boundary of existing GAAP and creativity beyond the boundary of existing GAAP.

Accounting policies define the process whereby transactions and other events are reflected in financial statements.[13] Management of an organization should select and consistently apply a set of accounting policies so that the financial statements comply with the GAAP and relevant legislation.[14] For example, an organization in Hong Kong holding inventories must account for its inventories in accordance with SSAP 22 of the HKICPA. Where there is no specific guidance in the GAAP, the management should use its judgement in developing accounting policies to ensure that the financial statements provide information that is: [15]

- relevant to the readers' needs and
- reliable in that they:
  - represent faithfully the results and financial position of the organization;
  - reflect the economic substance of events and transactions and not merely the legal form;
  - are neutral, that is free from bias;
  - are prudent; and
  - are complete in all material respects.

Where it is necessary to choose between accounting policies that satisfy the above conditions, an organization should select whichever of those accounting policies is judged by the organization to be most appropriate to its particular circumstances for the purpose of giving a true and fair view.[16] By manipulating the choice and application of accounting policies, perpetrators commit accounting irregularities.

The objectives against which an organization should judge the appropriateness of accounting policies to its particular circumstances are:[17]

- relevance
- reliability
- comparability
- understandability.

All of these four objectives are also referred to as the qualitative characteristics of financial information.[18] Let us briefly consider each of them.

Relevance

Information in the financial statements is relevant if it has the ability to influence the readers' economic decisions and is provided in time to influence those decisions. Decisions are about predicting the future and taking the appropriate steps to capture emerging opportunities and to mitigate associated risks. Without the predictive ability, information is irrelevant to readers, and perpetrators may want to mislead readers by adopting accounting policies which are irrelevant to the readers.

Reliability

Financial information is reliable if it represents faithfully what it is supposed to represent and reflects the substance of the underlying events and transactions.

Perpetrators may adopt certain unreliable measurements to advance their self-interests; for example some perpetrators may try to create hidden reserves or excessive provisions, deliberately understate assets or gains, or deliberately overstate liabilities or losses. Reliability hinges on an accounting concept, known as prudence (see a subsequent section), which requires a degree of caution in the exercise of judgement in uncertain situations during the preparation of financial statements. However, it is not necessary to exercise prudence where there is no uncertainty, otherwise the financial statements are not neutral and not reliable.

Comparability

Comparability implies consistency in an organization's financial statements within a financial year and from one financial year to the next.[19] Consistency is not the same as absolute uniformity, but it is useful in enhancing comparability between organizations. Comparability is also considered in the next section as part of a fundamental concept in financial reporting, namely *consistency*.

Understandability

Readers of financial statements should not be required to read between the lines. Appropriate choices of accounting policies result in financial information being presented in a way that enables its meaning and significance to be understood by readers. Complicated arrangements and complex accounting entries are often used by perpetrators to disguise or misrepresent the truth and to confuse the readers of financial statements.

FUNDAMENTAL CONCEPTS IN FINANCIAL REPORTING

The basis of preparation of financial statements relies on a number of fundamental concepts which effectively sets out the underlying assumptions of financial statements. Let us consider six fundamental concepts:

- going concern
- accruals (or matching)
- consistency (or comparability)
- prudence
- materiality
- offsetting.

GOING CONCERN

As one of the concepts adopted in FRS 18 of the ASB, the going-concern concept assumes that an organization will continue in existence for the foreseeable future. An organization should prepare its financial statements on a going-concern basis, unless:[20]

- the organization is being liquidated or has ceased trading; or

- the management has no realistic alternative but to liquidate the organization or to cease trading.

When preparing financial statements, the management should assess the organization's ability to continue as a going concern. When the management is aware of material uncertainties which may cast significant doubt upon the organization's ability to continue as a going concern, those uncertainties should be disclosed. When the financial statements are not prepared on a going-concern basis, the fact should be disclosed, together with the basis on which the financial statements are prepared and the reason why the organization is not considered to be a going concern.[21]

In assessing whether the going-concern assumption is appropriate, the management takes into account all available information for the foreseeable future (that is for a minimum period of 12 months from the financial year-end). For organizations which are profitable with good financial strength, the going-concern basis of accounting is obviously appropriate without the need for any detailed analysis. In other cases, a wider range of factors of consideration is required surrounding profitability, debt repayment schedules and potential sources of replacement financing before concluding whether the going-concern basis is appropriate.

When an organization suffers from severe losses and net deficits (liabilities exceed assets), perpetrators may still try to adopt the going-concern basis in order to avoid sending a negative message to readers. When readers become aware of the organization's inability to sustain the going-concern basis, they may decide to pull the plug and to withdraw their financial support. That would become a self-fulfilling prophecy maximizing the likelihood of the organization going bust. The results may be massaged in the perpetrators' favour through the good and bad years. Perpetrators may try setting aside certain unnecessary provisions which would only materialize if the organization in question was being wound up, such as provision for large-scale redundancy payments and other significant provisions (overstatement of liabilities – see Chapter 6).

Perpetrators may also try stating assets at their break-up value, which is not consistent with the going-concern concept. In some cases, by using an inappropriate valuation basis, perpetrators may want to portray a higher net worth for the organization in the financial statements. Financial statements are usually prepared on the basis that the organization is a going concern because measures based on break-up values tend to be irrelevant to readers seeking to assess the organization's operating capabilities, financial adaptability and cash generation ability.

ACCRUALS (OR MATCHING)

This concept requires the matching of costs to revenues, and bringing them into the profit and loss account in the financial year to which they relate. This means recognizing transactions and events when they occur (and not as cash is received or paid). Expenses are recognized in the P&L on the basis of a direct matching between revenue and the costs in producing that revenue. An organization should prepare its financial statements, except for cash flow information, on the accrual basis of accounting.[22] The accruals concept lies at the heart of definitions of assets and liabilities (see Chapter 5).

Figure 2.2 plots the first 40 years of an organization against the cumulative profits per its financial statements and attempts to illustrate the variation of the cut-off point in time when expenses and revenues are recognized in the financial statements. There are three possible variations regarding the cut-off recognition time. In Scenario A, the organization recognizes sales revenue as soon as its customers make the commitment (that is, at the point when the customers place the order). That is known as commitment accounting. Similarly, for commitments made by the organization (such as a signed contract to invest into a significant project), rather than disclosing

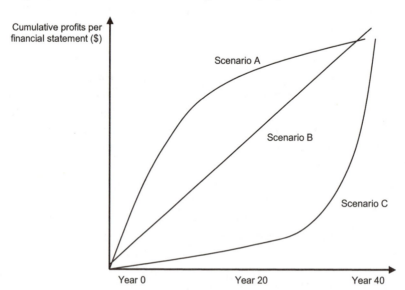

Figure 2.2   Cumulative profits over a 40-year period

commitments in the notes to the financial statements ('Notes'), they are recognized as liabilities at the point when the contract becomes effective. In Scenario B, the organization adopts the accrual basis in its financial statements. In Scenario C, the organization recognizes sales revenues upon the receipt of cash from its customers (cash accounting). No business lasts forever. Ultimately, over a long period of time, when the organization is terminated and no more transactions are outstanding, the cumulative profits for all three scenarios are the same.

However, the accruals concept does not allow the recognition of items in the B/S which do not meet the definition of assets or liabilities. For example, although advertisements are used with a view to equipping the organization with the capability to earn more revenues over the future financial year, it does not result in any identifiable resource from which those economic benefits are derived. Therefore, advertising costs should be recognized as an expense in the financial year in which they are incurred.

In addition, perpetrators may manipulate the cut-off of sales revenue (see *revocable sales* in Chapter 3) and apply irregular accounting techniques, such as *aggressive capitalization of expenditure* and *lax policy in charging expenses* as set out in Chapter 4.

CONSISTENCY (OR COMPARABILITY)

The usefulness of an organization's financial statements tends to increase if they can be compared with similar information about the organization in different financial years, and with similar information about other organizations.[23] Such comparability can usually be achieved through a combination of consistency of accounting method and of presentation.

By frequently changing the accounting method which gives the desired results within the GAAP, perpetrators are in violation of the consistency concept because, once chosen, the same accounting method should be consistently adopted. The basis of disclosure and classification of items in the financial statements should be retained from one financial year to the next unless: [24]

- a significant change in the nature of the organization's business and operation has occurred;

- the change will result in a more appropriate presentation of events or transactions after a review of the existing financial statement presentation; or

- a change in presentation is required by the appropriate GAAP.

An organization should change the presentation of its financial statements only if the revised structure is likely to continue, or if the benefit of an alternative presentation is clear. When such changes in presentation are made, an organization should also reclassify its comparative information.[25]

As discussed in the last section, comparability generally implies consistency throughout an organization's financial statements within each financial year and from one financial year to the next.[26] However, consistency is not a need for absolute uniformity and should not become an obstacle to improved accounting practices. In selecting accounting policies, an organization should assess whether the adopted industry practices are appropriate to its particular circumstances.

PRUDENCE

This concept is a reaction to the uncertainty arising from estimates and requires a degree of caution in the exercise of judgement in preparing financial statements. As one of the qualitative characteristics of financial statements, prudence is a factor to be considered in developing accounting policies to give reliable information.[27] Often there is uncertainty about the amount at which items in the financial statements should be measured. Prudence requires that accounting policies take account of such uncertainty in recognizing and measuring those assets, liabilities, gains, losses and changes to capital (shareholders' funds).

Although it is appropriate to exercise a degree of caution when dealing with uncertainties, the prudence concept cannot be used to justify the overstatement of liabilities or the understatement of assets and does not override the explicit requirements of other GAAP. Information in the financial statements should be neutral and free from bias.

Exercising the prudence concept is not required where there is no uncertainty.[28] It is also not appropriate to use prudence as an excuse for accounting irregularities, such as creating hidden reserves or excessive provisions, deliberately understating assets or gains, or deliberately overstating liabilities or losses.

MATERIALITY

The materiality concept asks whether the inclusion of the item in the financial statements enhances the usefulness of the financial statements in the eyes of the readers. Similar to relevance as one of the four qualitative characteristics of financial information, information in financial statements is material if the omission, misstatement or non-disclosure has the ability to influence the readers' economic decisions. Each material item should be presented separately in the financial statements.[29] Immaterial amounts may be aggregated with amounts of a similar nature or function and need not be presented separately.

In deciding whether an item of information is material, both the nature and size should be considered. For example, individual assets with the same nature and function are aggregated even if the individual amounts are large. However, large items which differ in nature or function are presented separately.

Materiality is the final test of what information should be given in a particular set of financial statements.[30] Materiality is therefore a threshold quality that is demanded of all information given in the financial statements. Furthermore, including immaterial information in financial statements may distract the attention of the readers from the critical information and impair the understandability of the financial statements as a whole. Perpetrators may try disclosing a large amount of immaterial data in the financial statements in order to divert the attention of the readers away from the key indicators. The *abuse of materiality concept* is considered in Chapter 7.

OFFSETTING

Assets and liabilities should not be offset unless the offsetting is required by the GAAP, legislation or when all the following conditions are met: [31]

- the organization and a counter-party owe each other a determinable monetary amount;

- the organization has the ability to insist on a net settlement. In determining this, any right to insist on a net settlement that is contingent should be taken into account only if the organization is able to enforce a net settlement by the counter-party; *and*

- the organization's ability to insist on a net settlement is assured beyond doubt. It is therefore necessary that the debit balance (receivables) matures no later than the credit balance (payables). It is also necessary that the organization's ability to insist on a net settlement would survive the insolvency of all of the parties involved.

It should be noted that presenting assets net of provisions or allowances, such as provisions for doubtful debts or inventory obsolescence, are not considered as offsetting.

In the UK, the Companies Act acknowledges the four fundamental accounting concepts of going concern, prudence, accruals and consistency, describing them as accounting principles, along with a fifth principle, known as the separate-valuation principle. In essence, the separate-valuation principle means no offsetting and states that, in determining the amount to be attributed to an asset or liability in the B/S, each item of assets or liabilities must be valued separately. These separate valuations are then totalled to arrive at the B/S figure.

When an organization and a counter-party owe each other certain amounts, the organization may be tempted to offset such amounts in the B/S. Similarly, for revenue and expense arising from the same or similar transactions, the organization may wish to offset such amounts in the P&L. This is so-called *aggressive offsetting* as described in Chapter 7.

Offsetting in either the P&L or the B/S, except when offsetting reflects the substance of the underlying transaction or event, detracts from the reader's ability to understand the transactions undertaken and to assess the future cash flows of the organization. Therefore, the circumstances in which such items may be offset are limited.[32]

Miscellaneous items (gains and losses) may be offset. This offsetting reporting may increase the likelihood that important information is overlooked in assessing financial performance. Typically, the net balance of these various miscellaneous items is simply presented on the face of the P&L. Notes to the financial statements are often not identified with this line item. Readers of financial statements should check the detail of the Notes, even in cases where the net balances are either small or relatively stable (because possibly their originating amounts could be very high and are significantly reduced due to the offsetting).

On the other hand, some perpetrators may avoid legitimate offsetting as part of a possible effort to portray an illusive picture of the organization. Let us consider a relevant case.

CASE 2.1

IRREGULAR REPORTING OF SALES RETURNS

P Ltd is an online retailer of books offering a 30-day free trial to customers. Sales returns from customers within 30 days of delivery can receive the full refunds. The level of sales returns is substantial at $2 million in 2004 against annual sales of $15 million. Sales returns effectively invalidate sales, and the two figures should be offset in the financial statements. However, in order to achieve good terms in a corporate buy and sell transaction, P Ltd wants a higher business valuation. As the value of P Ltd is perceived by the market at a multiple of sales revenue (rather than net profit), P Ltd is caught for boosting a high turnover and treating the $2 million sales returns as cost of sales.

How organizations report sales revenue for the goods and services they offer is becoming an increasingly important issue because some investors may value certain organizations on a multiple of revenues rather than a multiple of profit. An example relates to the way a principal's revenue is reported in the financial statements. If an organization simply acts as an agent for a principal, the sales revenue reported by the agent should only be the commission rather than the full amount of the underlying goods or services (which are included in the principal's financial statements). However, some perpetrators acting as an agent may fabricate documents to portray a different but irregular principal/agent relationship in supporting an overstatement of sales revenue.

DOUBLE-ENTRY BOOK-KEEPING AND ACCOUNTING EQUATION

Double-entry book-keeping can be traced back to the thirteenth century in Northern Italy. In 1494, a Franciscan monk Luca Pacioli was one of the first to publish the practice of double-entry book-keeping. Four centuries later, accountants started grouping together to form professional bodies, such as:

- The Institute of Chartered Accountants of Scotland (and its predecessor) in 1854

- The Institute of Chartered Accountants in England and Wales in 1880

- The American Institute of Certified Public Accountants (and its predecessor) in 1887.

The fundamental idea of double-entry book-keeping is that all monetary transactions shall be recorded twice as debit and credit in the accounts based on the principle that every monetary transaction involves the simultaneous receiving and giving of value.

An account refers to a specific way of categorizing similar transactions. All transactions are recorded in accounts that are labelled as:

- assets
- liabilities
- capital (or owners' equity)
- revenue
- expenditure.

Debits increase the accounts of assets and expenditure (such as buying a filing cabinet and incurring telephone expenses); credits decrease them. Conversely, credits increase liabilities, capital and revenue accounts (such as drawing a bank loan, issuing more shares and striking a sale); debits decrease them. Being in balance means that total debit entries equates to total credit entries. However, it does not prove that the accounts or financial statements are free from mis-statements and irregularities. Without upsetting the balance of the accounting system, perpetrators may still try disguising expenditure as assets (or vice versa) and revenue as liabilities (or vice versa).

Uncovering accounting irregularities often requires an understanding of the debits and credits. For example, a $10 000 cash shortfall may mean either a debit entry in the cash book without trace of the equivalence in the bank statement or a withdrawal in the bank statement not reflected in the cash book. In searching for the black hole, the accounting system is reviewed, and a debit in the legal expense account and a corresponding credit in the cash book for $10 000 are found without any supporting documentation. Based on the principle of double-entry book-keeping, it is plausible to suspect that the perpetrator may have attempted to conceal the theft (the credit in the cash book) by labelling the stolen $10 000 as a legal expense (the debit in the legal expense account).

If the accounts do not balance, there must be an error in recording the transactions or an accounting irregularity because one side of the accounting entries is missing. However, a balanced set of accounts does not guarantee the financial statements are free from mis-statement and accounting irregularities. In general, a balanced set of accounts may still contain the following types of errors:

- Omission – it refers to a complete omission of a transaction, because neither a debit nor a credit is made.

- Original entry – it refers to the wrong amount being debited and credited to the correct accounts.

- Commission – it refers to posting a transaction to the wrong account, although the right type of account; for example, the buying of petrol is debited to the heating and lighting account rather than motor expenses (both are expenditure accounts)

- Principle – it occurs when the wrong type of account is used, such as the purchase of a motor van being debited to an expenditure account (for example motor expenses) rather than a fixed assets account.

- Compensation – it refers to an error of, say, $10 being exactly compensated by another $10 error elsewhere.

Audit trail refers to the linkage between documents and accounting records enabling source documentation to be traced to financial statements and vice versa. Audit trail is a legal requirement[33] and is important to ensure transactions can be followed through to ensure their completeness and accuracy. Legitimate transactions leave an audit trail, while accounting irregularities may disguise the audit trail.

A good understanding of the audit trail through various steps of the accounting cycle is important in investigating accounting irregularities. They start with a source document such as an invoice, a cheque, a receipt or a received report. These source documents become the basis for accounting entries which are effectively the chronological listings of the debits and credits entries of transactions. Entries are made in various journals which are posted to the appropriate general ledger account. The summarized account amounts become the basis for financial statements for a particular financial year.

Regardless of what business an organization is in, the fundamental success factor is to buy at the minimum cost and to sell at the maximum price. Its transactions always flow with two main cycles:

- purchase and payment cycle
- sales and receipt cycle.

Purchase and payment cycle

The purchase and payment cycle typically starts with the initiation of a purchase requisition by someone who has a need for the goods or services (the user department) and ends with the record of a correct payment to the vendors.

The purchase and payment cycle can be summarized into six stages:

- needs for purchase arising
- placing the purchase order
- receiving the goods or services
- recording transactions in journals
- posting journals to individual accounts
- summarizing accounts and presenting them on to the financial statements.

The following documents and records can usually be found in the operation of a purchase and payment cycle.

- Purchase requisition – it is issued when there is a need arising in an organization. It is a request for goods or services by an authorized employee of the user department passing from the user department to the buying department.

- Purchase order – following the purchase requisition, an order is placed with the appropriate vendor for the necessary purchases. It is a properly authorized document from an organization to the vendor, recording the description, quantity and amount of the goods or services ordered.

- Goods receipt note – upon receipt of goods or services, the liability to pay has fallen on to the organization and the purchase is usually accrued in the accounts, particularly at the financial year-end. It is a document by an authorized employee of the receiving department at the time the goods are received, showing the description, quantity, condition and date of the goods received.

- Purchase invoice – the purchase is formally recognized in the total creditor account (converted from the accrual account). It is a document issued by the vendor, indicating the date, description, quantity and the total amount of goods and services specifying an organization's liability relating to the purchase.

- Purchase journal – it is a document for recording the purchases and serves as a posting summary to the accounting system.

- Purchase (creditors') ledgers – it is a subsidiary set of records of vendors' accounts which record individual purchases, cash payments, purchase returns and discounts.

- Payment voucher – it is accompanied with a purchase invoice, goods receipt note and/or purchase order for payment approval and establishes a formal means of recording and controlling cash disbursement. It also forms the basis of posting the cash disbursement into the accounting system.

- Cheque or electronic transfer – it is the actual payment to the vendors and signifies the cash outflow of an organization so that the proper authorized signatories are necessary.

- Remittance advice – it refers to a document sent with the cheques to a vendor, detailing the amount of payment for each corresponding invoice and the total amount paid.

- Vendor's statement – it refers to a statement prepared by the vendor, indicating the opening balance, purchases during the period, payments received by the vendor and closing balance. The closing balance of the vendor's statement should be the same as that recorded in the vendor's account in the purchase ledger except for timing differences and disputed amounts.

Sales and receipt cycle

The sales and receipt cycle starts with the receipt of an order from a customer (as received by the sales department) and ends with the record of a correct receipt from the relevant customer. The sales and receipt cycle can be summarized into six stages:

- customers' orders coming in
- producing the required goods or services
- dispatching the goods or services
- recording transactions in journals
- posting journals to individual accounts
- summarizing accounts and presenting them on to the financial statements.

The following documents and records can usually be found in the operation of a sales and receipt cycle.

- Customer order – it is a request for goods from a customer received by the sales department. It forms the basis for the organization's production.

- Sales order – it is sometimes issued in addition to the customer order as a document recording the description, quantity and related information of the goods or services ordered to confirm the order received. It is also used internally for credit approval and authorization for delivery of goods or services.

- Shipping document or delivery note – upon delivery of goods or services, the sale is usually recognized in the accounts, particularly at the financial year-end. It is a document prepared at the time when the goods are shipped or delivered, detailing the description, the quantity shipped and other relevant data.

- Sales invoice – it is a document indicating the details of goods sold, such as descriptions, quantity, terms of sales, unit price and the total amount billed for recording in the accounting records.

- Sales journal – it is a document for recording sales and serves as a posting summary to the accounting system.

- Credit note – it is raised as a result of approval for customers' returns or granting allowances to customers, and its function is like an invoice but acts in the opposite way in that it indicates the amount to be deducted from a customer's account.

- Remittance advice – it refers to a customer's document together with the payment indicating the customer's name and numbers, and the amounts of the individual invoices.

- Receipt – it is a document issued by the seller to the customer for acknowledgement of receipt of payment, detailing the numbers and amounts of individual sales invoices settled. Duplicated copies of receipts may be used as posting sources to individual debtors' accounts and the cash receipt journal. Some organizations may use a pay-in slip as the posting source instead.

- Cash receipt journal – it is a journal for recording cash receipts from cash sales, collections and all other cash received. Each individual entry is supported by either receipt copies or pay-in slips and the daily or monthly total is posted to the bank account and debtors' control account in the general ledger.

- Sales (debtors') ledger – it is a subsidiary set of records of customers' accounts for detailing individual sales, cash receipts, sales returns and discounts.

- Monthly statement – it refers to a document sent to each customer detailing the opening balance of the month, the movement of transactions during the month such as the amount and date of each sale, return and cash receipt, and the closing balance due.

ACCOUNTING EQUATION AND FINANCIAL STATEMENTS

Similar to the concept of debits equalling credits, the 'accounting equation' also forms the foundation of accounting and the double-entry book-keeping regime. The accounting equation is:

$$\text{Assets} = \text{Liabilities} + \text{Capital (owners' equity)}$$

The assets sides of the accounting equation consist of the net resources employed by an organization, such as property, equipment, inventory, receivables and cash, as well as intangible items of value such as patents, licences and trademarks. To qualify as an asset, an item provides future benefits and is owned by the organization in question. A full definition of assets is considered in Chapter 5.

Liabilities are an organization's obligations or an outsider's claim against an organization's assets. Liabilities are generally incurred through the acquisition of assets or by expenses not yet paid.

Capital (owners' equity) represents the owners' investment into the organization plus its retained profits (accumulated revenue less expenditure). From the equation, it can also be seen that capital is equal to assets minus liabilities.

Any transactions affecting the amount of total assets must also change liabilities and/or capital, and vice versa, except that a transaction may use up assets of a certain value to obtain other assets of the same value. For example, a business pays $1000 for some goods. Its total assets will be unchanged because the amount of cash falls by $1000 and the value of inventory rises by $1000. If an organization borrows from a bank, cash (asset) and bank loan (liability) increase to show the receipt of cash and an obligation owed by the organization. Since both assets and liabilities increase by the same amount, the equation stays in balance.

As introduced in Chapter 1 about the financial reporting environment with reference to the financial statements, the accounting equation can also help in explaining the interaction amongst the three of the four primary statements of the financial statements:

- B/S

- P&L

- Statement of changes in equity (or statement of total recognized gains and losses).

The B/S is effectively an extension of the accounting equation by listing assets, liabilities and capital. The capital in an organization usually can be viewed as from two sources – retained profits and owners' contributions (share capital). Retained profits increase when an organization has profits and decreases when an organization has losses or when there is a distribution of profits to the owners in the form of dividends. Share capital increases only when the owners invest in an organization. Thus, the basic accounting equation expands into:

$$\text{Assets} = \text{Liabilities} + \text{Share Capital} + \text{Retained Profits}$$

While a B/S shows total assets, liabilities and owners' equity at a specific point in time (usually the last day of a financial year), a P&L details how much profit (or loss) an organization has made during a financial year.

Two types of accounts are reported on the P&L – revenues and expenses. The format for P&L is:

$$\text{Profits} = \text{Revenues} - \text{Expenses}$$

At the end of each financial year, revenues and expenses are closed or brought to a zero balance and the difference, net profits (losses), are added to (or deducted from) retained profits on the B/S. The P&L ties to the B/S through the retained profits account as follows:

$$Assets = Liabilities + Share\ Capital + Retained\ Profits$$
$$(where\ Retained\ Profits = Profits - Dividends)$$

The accounting equation can be illustrated in Table 2.1, which contains six simple transactions of a newly established organization. The table shows that the $1200 assets equate to the $100 liabilities plus the $1000 share capital and the $100 retained profits.

Table 2.1   Illustration of the accounting equation

Transaction	Assets Debit/ (credit) $	Liabilities Debit/ (credit) $	Share capital Debit/ (credit) $	Profits Debit/ (credit) $	Dividends Debit/ (credit) $
Inject $1 000 share capital in cash	1 000 cash		(1 000)		
Buy $300 of goods on credit from a vendor		(300) creditor		300 purchase	
Pay $300 to the vendor	(300) cash	300 settlement			
Sell all the goods to a customer on credit for $500	500 debtors			(500) sales	
Receive $500 from the customer	500 cash (500) settlement				
Close the accounts and declare $100 as dividend		(100) dividend payable			100 declared dividend
	1 200	(100)	(1 000)	(200)	100

CONCLUSION

Accounting may be regarded as an information-processing system that is used to classify and record monetary transactions and to present the financial results of an organization for the readers of financial statements to make decisions. Due to irregular accounting practices, an organization's affairs and financial positions often look very different to the picture painted by the financial statements.

Accounting irregularities defeat the purposes of accounting and take various forms, but they all violate the GAAP and relevant legislations in favour of the perpetrators in question. However, the basics of accounting irregularities largely rest on three grounds:

- concealment or fabrication of genuine transactions or documents
- abuse of fundamental concepts in financial reporting
- manipulation of double-entry book-keeping entries.

Notes

1, 2, 3, 4 – *Towards the Third Dimension of Financial Reporting: Mandatory Disclosure of Corporate Forecasts*, pages 11 and 12, 1993 (an unpublished paper by Benny K. B. Kwok, University of Southampton, UK)

5, 6, 7 – SAS 110 *The Auditors' Responsibility to Consider Fraud and Error in an Audit of Financial Statements* (issued by the HKICPA in February 2002, effective for audits of financial statements for periods ending on or after 31 March 2002)

6 – SAS 110 *Fraud and Error* (issued by the APB in January 1995, effective for audits of financial statements for accounting periods ending on or after 30 June 1995)

8, 14, 15, 21, 22, 24, 25, 29, 31, 32 – SSAP 1 *Presentation of Financial Statements* (issued by the HKICPA in March 1984, revised May 1999, August 2001 and December 2001 effective for accounting periods starting on or after 1 January 2002)

9, 13, 16, 17, 20, 21, 22, 23 – FRS 18 *Accounting Policies* (issued by the ASB in December 2000, effective for accounting periods ending on or after 22 June 2001)

10, 11, 12 – *Towards the Third Dimension of Financial Reporting: Mandatory Disclosure of Corporate Forecasts*, pages 25 and 26, 1993 (an unpublished paper by Benny K. B. Kwok, University of Southampton, UK)

18, 19, 26, 28, 30 – The ASB, *Statement of Principles for Financial Reporting* (issued in December 1999)

27 – The HKICPA, *Framework for the Preparation and Presentation of Financial Statements* (issued in June 1997 and revised in May 2003)

33 – The Companies Ordinance, Hong Kong
The Companies Act, UK

CHAPTER 3

Selling More

OVERSTATEMENT OF SALES REVENUE

'Selling more' is what drives some perpetrators. By overstating the sales of an organization, perpetrators try to create a selling-more illusion – fabricating that the organization appears to have made more sales than it genuinely has. Defining the correct figure of sales revenue of goods or services should be done with reference to the appropriate generally accepted accounting principles (GAAP). Any departures from these are deemed to be irregular (accounting irregularities).

Sales are usually the largest item in a profit and loss account of most organizations. Sales figures provide a good indication of the activity level and capacity of the organization in question.

In recent years, it has become common for investors in certain industries and start-up organizations to focus on sales growth and acceleration as a reflection of an organization's potential. It was a typical phenomenon in 1999–2000 when the organizations with exposure to the Internet were valued at multiples of their sales regardless of their profits or losses. While these dot-com organizations reported recurring losses, the market believed that as long as sales revenue continued to grow rapidly, profits would materialize eventually ... until the bubble burst in the spring of 2000.

Appearing on the first row in the profit and loss account (P&L), the sales figure tends to attract a significant level of attention from the readers of financial statements and has a direct impact on the net profit. Therefore, it is often regarded as one of the most sensitive reported amounts as far as the financial statements are concerned. Indeed, accounting irregularities involving overstatement of sales have the dual purpose of portraying a selling-more illusion and inflating the organization's profitability.

Turnover, income, revenue, gains and sales revenue (or simply sales) are similar terms and, if loosely defined, may be used interchangeably. Strictly speaking, sales arise from the delivery of goods or the provision of services and are a subset of income or revenue. Other than those in certain specific industries (such as banks, charities and investment holding institutions), the main sources of income or revenue for most organizations are from sales.

RELEVANT GAAP IN HONG KONG AND THE UK

In Hong Kong, there are two main reference points for the accounting treatment of sales. The first one is the *Framework for the Preparation and Presentation of Financial Statements* (Framework) issued by the HKICPA in June 1997 (revised May 2003). Also, the HKICPA issued SSAP 18 *Revenue* in September 1995 (revised January and May 2001) effective for the accounting periods ending on or after 31 December 1995. Under the Framework and SSAP 18, income is largely defined as increases in economic benefits during the accounting period in the form of enhancements of assets (or decreases of liabilities) other than capital or equity contributions. In this context, income includes both revenue and gains.

Revenue is included in the definition of income that arises from an organization's ordinary activities and may be called sales, fees, interest, dividends, royalties and rent. Gains represent increases in economic benefits that meet the definition of income and are often reported net of related expenses; for example net exchange gains, net gains on disposal of assets. There are also unrealized gains, such as a revaluation of investment in securities. To sum up, SSAP 18 of the HKICPA only deals with the type of income which is revenue arising from:

- the sales of goods;
- the rendering of services; or
- the use of the organization's assets by others which pays interest, royalties and dividends.

In the UK, the ASB issued *Statement of Principles for Financial Reporting* in December 1999 (Principles). Gains are defined as increases in ownership interest not resulting from contributions from owners and incorporate all forms of income and revenue as well as all recognized gains (realized and unrealized) on non-revenue items. The Principles regard ownership interest as the residual amount found by deducting all of the organization's liabilities (obligations to give economic benefits) from all of the organization's assets (rights to receive future economic benefits).

The ASB also issued an attachment to FRS 5 *Substance of Transactions* in November 2003, known as Appendix G *Reporting the Substance of Transactions: Revenue Recognition* (FRS 5-G). FRS 5-G states that a seller recognizes revenue under an exchange of transactions with a customer when, and to the extent that, it obtains the right to consideration in exchange for its performance. At the same time, it typically recognizes a new asset, usually a debtor.

The primary issue in accounting for revenue relates to the timing of recognition, that is, deciding at which point the revenue in question is recorded in the P&L. This chapter mainly focuses on sales, but it is important to bear in mind that other types of income or revenue (such as interests, royalties, dividends and exchange gains) are also vulnerable to accounting irregularities and are subject to similar underlying principles.

The concept of 'substance over form' requires looking into the commercial substance of the underlying transaction(s).[1] Amounts collected on behalf of third parties such as sales taxes, goods and services taxes and value added taxes are not economic benefits which flow to the organization and are excluded from revenue. In the context of the selling arrangement between agents and principals, the amounts collected on behalf of the principal are not revenue, and only the amount of commission is regarded as revenue in the agent's P&L. Where the seller acts as principal, it should report turnover based on gross amount received or receivable in return for its performance under the contractual arrangement.[2] When the seller acts as agent, it should only report turnover as the commission receivable in return for its performance under the contractual arrangement.

For sales revenue to be recognized,[3]

- the seller must have transferred to the buyer the significant risks and rewards of ownership of the goods or service deliverables;

- the seller must not retain managerial involvement and/or effective control over the goods sold or service delivered;

- the amount of revenue must be measured reliably;

- it is probable that the seller will receive the economic benefits;

- the costs of the transaction must be measured reliably; *and*

- the stage of completion of the service deliverables at the financial year-end must be measured reliably.

SSAP 18 is adopted from the International Accounting Standard 18 *Revenue* (revised 1993) (IAS 18). There is no significant difference between the two standards. Although less comprehensive in scope, FRS 5-G is consistent with IAS 18.

RECOGNITION AND MEASUREMENT OF SALES

Having reviewed the appropriate GAAP in Hong Kong and the UK together with a brief comparison to the relevant IAS, there are four common grounds for the recognition and measurement of sales, as follows:

- Sales are gross inflows of economic benefits from buyers to sellers.

- Sales are transfers of the significant risks and rewards of goods or service deliverables from sellers to buyers.

- Sales are final and unconditional, and sellers have no more influence and/or control over the goods or service deliverables.

- Sales are quantifiable, and the amount can be measured reliably.

Sales revenue of an organization may be visualized along a timescale as set out in Figure 3.1. Let us assume that the correct sales for the organization in question are $100 million for each of the three years (2004, 2005 and 2006) in accordance with the relevant GAAP. This gives a total of $300 million for the three years combined. Perpetrators may fabricate two types of accounting irregularity to distort the total figure of $300 million and/or its allocation amongst the three years.

Figure 3.1   Sales revenue timescale

Firstly, perpetrators may try creating fictitious sales, and the total $300 million sales of the three-year period could be overstated by so-called phantom sales. For the second type of accounting irregularity, perpetrators may try buying more time and fiddling with the recognition criteria of genuine sales by shifting the whole or part of the $100 million sales from year to year. As a result, the organization's sales revenue and profit for one particular year could be inflated at the expense of another financial year's sales and profit. The three-year total remains intact because 'revocable sales' by definition would be reversed in other financial years. In essence, perpetrators 'borrow' sales from other financial years and record them in the current year.

ACCOUNTING IRREGULARITIES

Accounting irregularities involving overstatements of sales can therefore be categorized as:

- phantom sales, and

- revocable sales.

Before considering each of them in turn, it should be stressed that the choice (or change) of the financial year-end by itself might have an unwarranted intent. The economic cycle of an organization varies according to its business nature (for example, an ice-cream business generates most of its sales during the summer), and some may well extend beyond a 12-month period. By skilfully choosing and/or changing the financial year-end, perpetrators impose artificial cut-offs and are able to manipulate the timing of the reported sales.

PHANTOM SALES

Phantom sales are simply fictitious revenue which involves the recording of non-existent goods or service deliverables. Phantom sales often involve the creation of dummy customers. Sales invoices and other supporting documents (such as orders and delivery notes) are forged to dummy customers and are recorded as a typical sales transaction in the accounts of sales and debtors respectively. Let us consider the following case.

CASE 3.1

FICTITIOUS SHIPMENT OF GOODS TO DUMMY CUSTOMERS

Shortly before the financial year-end in 2004, a company of perpetrators (P Ltd) issues an invoice to a dummy customer (Dummy) for a fictitious shipment of goods worth $850 000. P Ltd makes the following accounting entries at the transaction date of 20 December 2004:

Dr		Trade debtors – Dummy	$850 000	
	Cr	Sales		$850 000

In closing the accounts on 31 December 2004, the $850 000 sales may not be questioned because the transaction and trade debt were both current (assuming all customers of P Ltd have a 30-day payment term). Dummy does not pay of course, and these fictitious entries are bound to surface during the subsequent audit in 2005. The receivable of $850 000 in Dummy's account is therefore found as irrecoverable and requires a write-off.

A detailed scrutiny on the receivable balance would reveal the fictitious sales. Therefore, P Ltd may try mixing the accounting irregularity with a variety of other tricks, such as using cash from a legitimate customer to cover the shortfalls in Dummy's account. If it is supported by cash inflows (which may well be a deposit from a legitimate customer), the accounting irregularity in Dummy's account is less likely to be caught, at least in the short term.

In some cases, legitimate customers are dragged into phantom sales.

CASE 3.2

PHANTOM SALES TO LEGITIMATE CUSTOMERS

Mr P is the sales director of a company and arranges the issue of some sale invoices in the name of a legitimate customer for items never sold or delivered. Those invoices are intercepted and withheld by Mr P himself. Without subsequent cash flows into the company, the phantom sales surface initially as a dispute with the legitimate customer. An investigation of the dispute reveals the truth, and Mr P is caught. Some perpetrators may reverse the phantom sales at the beginning of the next financial year thus concealing the accounting irregularities, but this will lead to a sales shortfall in the new financial year, creating the need for more phantom sales.

Another trick involving legitimate customers may well be to artificially inflate or alter invoices, reflecting higher amounts or quantities than actually sold. Mr P mixes genuine sold items with items not ordered by customers in invoices, hoping that invoices and monthly statements are not checked before payments. In extreme cases, perpetrators fabricate the unsupported sales and book the revenues in the hope that questions are not asked about the missing documentation.

Let us consider four cases of accounting irregularities of phantom sales involving bribery and conspiracy.

CASE 3.3

PHANTOM SALES MIXING WITH INFLATED SALES AND INTER-COMPANY TRANSFERS

A company of perpetrators (P Ltd) enters into a secret arrangement with an unrelated company (Customer A1) which agrees to 'buy' $100 000 worth of goods from P Ltd. However, there is no delivery of goods and this $100 000 transaction is a case of phantom sales because P Ltd agrees to pay $110 000 to Customer A2 (which is related to Customer A1) for goods with a market value of merely $80 000. In other words, P Ltd accepts goods worth $80 000 but pays Customer A2 $110 000. Out of the $110 000, Customer A2 pays $103 000 to Customer A1.

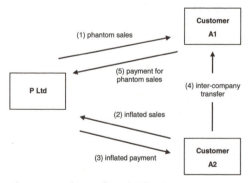

Figure 3.2   Phantom sales, inflated sales, inter-company transfers

Stage 1 – Phantom sales of $100 000 from P Ltd to Customer A1
Stage 2 – Inflated sales of $110 000 for $80 000 worth of goods from Customer A2 to P Ltd
Stage 3 – Payment of $110 000 from P Ltd to Customer A2
Stage 4 – Inter-company transfer of $103 000 from Customer A2 to Customer A1
Stage 5 – Payment of $100 000 from Customer A1 to P Ltd as settlement of phantom sales

In essence, P Ltd offers a bribe of $10 000 ($110 000 less $100 000) to induce phantom sales of $100 000, which is subsequently supported by cash flow from an apparently genuine customer, Customer A2. However, this accounting irregularity surfaces during the evaluation of closing inventories, and a write-down/provision of $20 000 ($100 000 less $80 000) is required to adjust the book value of the inventories in question to its recoverable amount (that is, the lower of costs of $100 000 and the net realizable value of $80 000). The bribe of $10 000 is split between Customer A1 and Customer A2 at $3000 and $7000, respectively. Customer A2 also earns the normal profits as derived from the sales of $80 000 worth of goods (although not quantified in this case).

CASE 3.4

PHANTOM SALES AND DEBT SETTLEMENTS IN A TRIPARTITE ARRANGEMENT

A company of perpetrators (P Ltd) makes 'sales' (which are in fact phantom sales) totalling $300 000 to its distributor (Distributor X). Distributor X agrees to pay for the phantom sales provided that P Ltd settle a debt of $305 000 on its behalf with an unrelated company (Vendor Y). P Ltd therefore places a sham order with Vendor Y and sends a cheque of $305 000 to Vendor Y. Vendor Y is not aware of the sham order and understands that the cheque is for the settlement of Distributor X's debt. Distributor X then pays $300 000 to P Ltd as settlement of phantom sales.

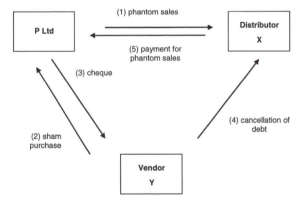

Figure 3.3 Phantom sales, debt settlement, tripartite arrangement

Stage 1 – Phantom sales of $300 000 from P Ltd to Distributor X

Stage 2 – Sham purchases of $305 000 from Vendor Y to P Ltd

Stage 3 – Payment of $305 000 from P Ltd to Vendor Y

Stage 4 – Acknowledgment of receipt of the $305 000 cheque for debt owed by Distributor X

Stage 5 – Payment of $300 000 from Distributor X to P Ltd as settlement of phantom sales

In essence, P Ltd offers bribe of $5000 to Distributor X ($305 000 less $300 000) to induce phantom sales of $300 000, which is subsequently supported by its own cash flow via Distributor X. However, this accounting irregularity surfaces during the evaluation of closing inventories as soon as the $305 000 amount of inventories shortfalls (a sham purchase from Vendor Y) is discovered.

CASE 3.5

DISGUISING A LIQUIDATION OF FIXED ASSETS

P Ltd is a catering business which includes door-to-door pizza delivery services. P Ltd sells a fleet of motor bikes, which is a fixed asset of P Ltd's accounts, and receives $400 000 from Buyer X which is unrelated.

In an attempt to impress its shareholders with rocketing sales revenue, P Ltd irregularly treats this disposal as sales proceeds from a restaurant chain for the pizza supplies over a six-month contract. Corresponding contract and sales invoices are fabricated. However, to maintain the door-to-door pizza delivery services, P Ltd requires a replacement fleet and therefore leases a number of motor bikes from Lessor Y. P Ltd pays a monthly lease payment of $8500 to Lessor Y and disguises it as sundry expenses, having convinced Lessor Y to alter the description of the invoices.

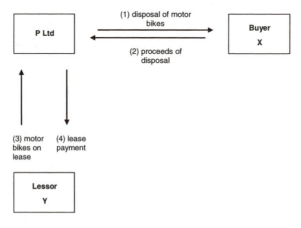

Figure 3.4   Disguising disposal of motor bikes

Stage 1 – Disposal of motor bikes from P Ltd to Buyer X

Stage 2 – Payment of $400 000 from Buyer X to P Ltd (phantom sales)

Stage 3 – Lease of a fleet of motor bikes from Lessor Y to P Ltd (cover-up of motor bikes)

Stage 4 – Monthly rent of $8500 from P Ltd to Lessor Y (sundry expenses)

In essence, P Ltd's sales are inflated by $400 000 which is the proceeds from the disposal of fixed assets and should have been included in the calculation of gains or losses as supported by cash receipt. The monthly lease of $8500 for the replacement bikes is hidden in sundry expenses and may be broken up in many tranches of payments scattered in a variety of expenditure accounts, each of which on its own is immaterial in the context of P Ltd's P&L. Eventually, this accounting irregularity is discovered when the registration numbers of the motor bikes are checked and found to be different from the records in P Ltd's fixed assets register.

CASE 3.6

CONSPIRACY OF A 'PERFECT COUPLE'

Mr P and Mrs P are husband and wife. Mr P is the owner of a company (P Ltd). Mrs P is a senior employee of an unrelated company. Mrs P uses her employer's stationery to issue a purchase order of $1m to P Ltd shortly before the financial year-end in 2001. Mrs P intercepts an audit confirmation from P Ltd's auditors and signs it with her maiden name. Mrs P's employer does not pay P Ltd, and the phantom sales are reversed in P Ltd's accounts in February 2002. As P Ltd's auditors only review subsequent transactions taking place during January, the reversal entries remain hidden.

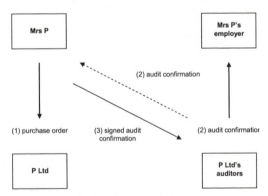

Figure 3.5 Conspiracy of a 'perfect couple'

Stage 1 – Purchase order of $1m from Mrs P's employer (upon Mr P's instructions) to P Ltd

Stage 2 – Audit confirmation from P Ltd's auditors to Mrs P's employer (intercepted by Mrs P)

Stage 3 – Signed audit confirmation from Mrs P to P Ltd's auditors

> The sales of P Ltd are overstated by $1 million (although reversed in the next financial year) in the financial year of 2001. This accounting irregularity is repeated a few times at each of the three subsequent financial year-ends and is only discovered in 2004 when the repeated pattern of sales reversal is questioned and investigated during the analytical review of the monthly sales figures.

REVOCABLE SALES

Phantom sales refer to fictitious, non-existent sales, but revocable sales are not fictitious. Revocable sales refer to sales which are provisional and incomplete and can therefore be revoked, cancelled or subject to some further negotiations or outstanding activities. An example of revocable sales involves premature recognition of sales, that is, recording a legitimate sale in a financial year before that called for by relevant GAAP. Perpetrators may also leave the books and accounts open for an excessively long time after the financial year-end in order to record sales that are taking place after the year-end. This is called manipulations of cut-offs.

From time to time, many organizations face surplus or unwanted inventories, which may be returned to suppliers for refunds. However, documents may be fabricated, changing the nature of the cash inflow from refunds to revenue. This particular type of accounting irregularity has no impact on the net profit because the refunds would otherwise be set off against the costs of goods sold. Some similar window-dressing techniques are used on sales of services particularly when the debtor is part of or related to the organization in question. Sales revenue from service deliverables are booked just before the financial year-end (such as fees for consultancy work) which may well be reversed soon after the year-end.

Sales to intermediate entities, such as distributors, dealers or other resalers, are often cited as other examples of revocable sales. As with other types of sales, they are generally recognized when the risks and rewards of ownership of goods or service deliverables have passed. When the buyer is acting, in substance, as an agent of the seller to sell the goods, these sales are really consignment sales which are revocable. Accordingly, no sales should be recognized by the seller until the goods are sold by the buyer to a third party.

Similarly, there are cases where the seller makes some sales but concurrently agrees to repurchase the same goods at a later date. In essence, the seller exercises a call option to repurchase, or the buyer exercises a put option to resell to the seller of the same goods. In considering these sale and repurchase agreements, it is critical to assess the precise moment that the transfer of the risks and rewards of ownership to the buyer is taking place. When the seller has retained the risks and rewards of ownership, even though legal title has been transferred, the transaction is a financing arrangement and does not give rise to sales revenue.

The main features of a sale and repurchase agreement are:[4]

- the sale price may be market value or another agreed price;
- the nature of the repurchase provision may be unconditional, an option for the seller to repurchase (a call option) and/or an option for the buyer to resell to the seller (a put option); *and*
- the repurchase price may be fixed or variable.

Sometimes this kind of sales and repurchase agreement may be in a slightly different form. For example, a sales transaction may appear to be a legitimate order from a creditworthy customer, but, looking closely, there is an attachment to the agreement (sometimes known as a 'side letter') which effectively neutralizes the transaction between buyer and seller.

It is normal commercial practice to have attachments that are used to clarify or modify terms of a sales transaction without undermining the agreement as a whole. The problem with some attachments arises when they are kept secret from the official books and records and are used to neutralize some of the disclosed terms of transaction. Examples of attachments which could invalidate the sales in question include: offering extensive rights to return or to cancel orders at any time; and introducing a break clause to cover various contingencies which makes the sale null and void or waives the payment if the goods purchased are not resold.

The dividing line between phantom sales and revocable sales is not often clear and can be illustrated in the following case.

CASE 3.7

PREMATURE RECORDING OF SALES

P Ltd receives a customer's order worth $700 000 with a delivery scheduled on 5 January 2005. The corresponding dispatch notes and transportation documentation have been amended to 30 December 2004 and P Ltd recognized the sales of $700 000 in the financial year-ended 31 December 2004. Although the sales in question are genuine, the transaction is recorded prematurely.

Rather than recording sales for goods not yet delivered as in this case, P Ltd could take more aggressive action by recognizing the sales revenue in advance of an order which is forthcoming. Given the lack of an actual order, such an act could fall into the category of phantom sales. As soon as the expected order is received, the transaction in question becomes a premature recognition of sales. In going even further than recognizing sales prior to an expected order, P Ltd could have recorded sales for which orders are not expected. Sales recognized in such situations would be considered fictitious, which falls into the category of phantom sales.

Some sales carry outstanding obligations or additional terms that have not been completed. The risks and rewards of ownership have not been passed to buyers and they must not be recognized as sales. These types of sales are manipulations of cut-offs since the conditions for sale will most likely be satisfied in the future, at which time the recognition of sales revenue would become appropriate. Let us consider two relevant cases.

CASE 3.8

DELIVERY AND INSTALLATION

P Ltd sells escalators and lifts. The sale agreement covers installation and inspection. The installation is a core part of the contract but P Ltd recognizes sales immediately upon the customers' acceptance of delivery. However, the risks and rewards of ownership do not pass until the installation is completed even though the goods have been delivered to the customer.

The correct treatment for P Ltd is to recognize sales when the customer accepts delivery, and installation and inspection have been completed. However, P Ltd may recognize sales immediately upon the customer's acceptance of delivery only if:[5]

- the installation process is simple in nature; for example, the installation of a factory-tested television receiver only requires unpacking and connection of power and antennae;
- the inspection is performed only for purposes of final determination of contract prices, such as shipments of iron ore, sugar or soya beans; or
- the customer has negotiated a limited right of return.

CASE 3.9

TRIAL PURCHASE

A company of perpetrators (P Ltd) is a computer software producer that operates a trial-run scheme for customers. The software is recorded as sales at the point when the customer accepts the trial-run. However, the sales contract offers the right of cancellation to the customer at the end of the trial-run. P Ltd is uncertain about the customers' return rate. Sales should not be recognized until after the lapse of the cancellation clause.[6]

This should be contrasted with the situation of a retailer that offers a refund policy for its customers. Since the retailer is usually in a position to predict the probability of goods returned on the basis of previous experience, revenue is recognized at the point of sale subject to the deduction of a reasonable estimate of the returns.

Revenue from property sales is normally recognized when legal title passes to the buyer. However, the equitable interest in a property (that is, the risks and rewards of ownership) may be transferred to the buyer before legal title passes. On the other hand, if the seller has further substantial acts to complete under the contract, it may not be appropriate to recognize revenue. A property may be sold with a degree of continuing involvement by the seller such that the risks and rewards of ownership have not been transferred. For example, the seller guarantees occupancy of the property for a specified period, or a rental return on the buyer's investment for a specified period. In such cases, the nature and extent of the seller's continuing involvement determines how the transaction is accounted for. Let us consider a relevant case.

CASE 3.10

IRREGULAR ACCOUNTING OF SALES OF PROPERTIES

A company of perpetrators (P Ltd) is a property developer in the UK which has been selling houses and apartments on one of its sites in Central London (London Houses) to overseas investors in Hong Kong (HK Investors). P Ltd guarantees an annual rental income return of 14 per cent for the first two years and undertakes to buy back the property if this return is not achieved (in fact, P Ltd is more likely to top up the rental shortfall rather than to fulfil the buy-back clause). However, it appears that the selling price of London Houses is 5–10 per cent above the market rate.

P Ltd sells London Houses to HK Investors totalling $10 million of which the market value is approximately $9–9.5 million. The annual rental income guarantee to HK Investors is $2.8 million (= $10 m × 14% × 2 years) over two years. However, the rental market in Central London only warrants a rent return of 10 per cent per annum which means an excess of 4 per cent per annum (= 14% – 10%), or $0.8 million over the first two years. This case can be illustrated in the following three-stage diagram.

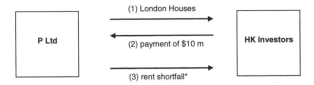

* to be filled by P Ltd, i.e., the difference between the guaranteed rent and the actual rent (assumed to be $0.8 m over two years

Figure 3.6   Irregular accounting of sales of properties, rental guaranteed

Stage 1 – London Houses are sold from P Ltd to HK Investors
Stage 2 – $10 million is paid from HK Investors to P Ltd
Stage 3 – Rent shortfall as guaranteed by P Ltd is paid to HK Investors

P Ltd recognizes the $10 million as sales at the time of the transfer of the legal title of London Houses. There is a shortfall in rent (borne by P Ltd) representing the difference between the guaranteed rent of $2.8 million (14 per cent per annum) and the (assumed) actual rent of $2 million (10 per cent per annum). Because of the buy-back clause, unless there is a two-year tenancy with an annual rent return of above 14 per cent per annum, P Ltd retains an obligation for unsatisfactory performance which, in essence, means the sales transaction has not yet been completed and should not be recognized.

Since P Ltd still retains the significant risks and rewards of ownership, the sales in question should be deferred. However, it is quite clear that the risks to P Ltd are limited to the rental shortfall of $0.8 million ($2.8 million less $2 million) of which a provision is set up in the same way as a retention or rebates payable to HK Investors. The provision can be released upon the lapse of the two-year period when P Ltd's buy-back obligation ends. As a result of the $10 million revocable sales, the accounting entries and relevant impacts may be as follows:

Accounting irregularities: revocable sales

Dr		B/S: Debtors	$10 m	
	Cr	P& L: Sales		$10 m

Correct accounting entries: at transaction date

Dr		B/S: Debtors	$10 m	
	Cr	B/S: Provision for rental guarantee		$0.8 m
	Cr	P&L: Sales		$9.2 m

Correct accounting entries: at the end of the second year (if there are no rental shortfalls)

Dr		B/S: Provision for rental guarantee	$0.8 m	
	Cr	P&L: Sales		$0.8 m

In some cases, the delivery of goods is delayed at the customer's request but the customer takes title and accepts billing. This is often referred to as 'bill and hold' sales. Revenue is recognized when the buyer takes title, provided that:

- it is probable that delivery will be made;
- the item is on hand, identified and ready for delivery to the buyer at the time the sale is recognized;
- the buyer specifically acknowledges the deferred delivery instructions; *and*
- the usual payment terms apply.

Revenue is not recognized when there is simply an intention to acquire or manufacture the goods in time for delivery. Let us consider a relevant case.

CASE 3.11

TITLE OF GOODS

P Ltd is a manufacturer of power generators offering one standard model and tailor-made generators at customers' specifications. Contracts for the standard models include P Ltd's specifications. Deposits of 10 per cent are required upon entering into the contract. If the generators do not perform to the specifications, a full refund is provided upon the return of the generators. Customers' acceptance (for a standard model) is confirmed in writing, or by implication following the lapse of 60 days from installation and test. Title to the equipment passes upon delivery to customers. Payment is due 30 days after delivery.

For tailor-made generators manufactured to customers' specification, 25 per cent deposits are required upon entering into the contract. Completed generators are inspected by customers. After acceptance by the customers, the sets ordered are held in a designated area in P Ltd's factory until the customers' delivery instructions. Payment for the 75 per cent balance is due 30 days after acceptance and transfer to the secured area. Title of goods does not pass to the customer until the generators are transferred out from the designated area for shipping (or the settlement date, if earlier).

It is P Ltd's accounting policy to recognize the sales of generators (standard or tailor-made models) upon the receipt of deposits. However, this accounting irregularity is later exposed and an accounting adjustment of a substantial sum is required, shifting the sales forward until the appropriate and later points of recognition.

The sales of standard model sets should be recognized upon delivery. In this case, title to the generators passes to customers upon delivery. Even though customers are entitled to a full refund before formal acceptance, the key question is whether P Ltd is able to assess the probability of goods returned based on previous experience. Unless it is likely that the generator will not perform in accordance with P Ltd's own specifications, it is appropriate for P Ltd to adopt a policy to recognize sales on delivery and before the customer's formal acceptance, particularly if P Ltd is responsible for the installation and testing of the equipment for the customers. However, the contractual terms for refund may create a legal obligation on P Ltd. The question of whether a provision for the expected returns should be made is to be considered in Chapter 6 (see Case 6.1).

For tailor-made generators, P Ltd should recognize the sales as and when the generators are transferred to the designated area which reflects the transfer of the significant risks and rewards of ownership to customers.

Since the generators are inspected and accepted by customers and are held in a designated area separate from P Ltd's own inventories, these sets can be considered as having been delivered to customers (although physically the generators are temporarily kept in P Ltd's factory). Payment for the balance within 30 days after acceptance and transfer to the designated area both provide further support of the point of revenue recognition being appropriate at the time of the transfer of generators to the designated areas.

Revenue cannot be recognized unless the amount of revenue to be received can be reliably measured.[7] In most cases, consideration will be agreed in advance, and the revenue from a sale will be recognized when all of the other recognition criteria are met.

Let us consider a case of car repairs at a garage.

CASE 3.12

PREMATURE RECOGNITION OF MOTOR INSURANCE CLAIMS

A car driver (Driver X), who is covered by his insurance, damages his car in an accident. Driver X takes his car to Garage P for repairs and claims against his insurer (Insurer Y). Garage P completes the repair and immediately raises an invoice for $20 000. The components are charged at list price whereas the labour hours are billed at the full rate, regardless of the adopted practice of 15 per cent discount for insurers and 10 per cent discount for walk-in and other retail customers.

Garage P recognizes the sales upon the issue of its invoice (as the list price) which, in this case, is shortly before its financial year-end and is not in accordance with the adopted practice of 15 per cent discount. After the financial year-end, the value of the invoice is reduced upon Insurer Y's payment which is based on the agreed items of works at the discounted rate. Adjustments to the sales figure (reduction of $3000) are made upon Insurer Y's payment, and P Ltd is caught practising this sales recognition policy for all of its repairs on insurance claims (which caused a larger impact on P Ltd's financial statements with some $200 000 of overstatement of sales).

Before sales are recognized, the price must be fixed or determinable, and many sales transactions contain an agreed price for the goods or services. In this case, the discount agreement between Garage P and Insurer Y, rather than the full list price, determines the amount of the reported sales revenue.

In the absence of an agreed price, revenue can be recognized when the price is set and is not subject to refunds or adjustments. For practical purposes, when services are performed by a series of indistinguishable acts over a specified period of time, revenue is recognized on a straight-line basis over the specified period unless there are some other methods to represent the stage of completion more accurately.

Let us consider a case about the subscription earned by a membership-based club. While a membership fee is paid up front, this type of club normally allows customers to cancel their membership at any time during a membership term for a full refund of the fee paid.

CASE 3.13

CLUB MEMBERSHIP SUBSCRIPTION

Club P is a club providing yoga lessons, with the membership subscription as its major source of income. An annual membership subscription is paid upfront for the use of the club's facilities and attendance at yoga lessons. Club P allows members to cancel their membership at any time during the year for a pro-rated refund of the subscription paid. Club P recognizes the sales upon the receipt of subscriptions.

For membership subscription or items of similar value in each time period, sales should be deferred and recognized over the period in which the items are delivered or provided.[8] Therefore, Club P should change this cash basis to accrual basis so that the annual subscription is deferred for recognition over the respective time period (12 months) covered by the membership agreement.

When a specific action or event is much more significant than any other matter, the recognition of revenue should be postponed until that significant action is completed.

It is often the case that a contractual arrangement may require the payment of a fee at inception which permits the customer to purchase goods or services over a period of time.[9] In determining when revenue should be recognized, the seller should determine whether or not the fee and the charges for goods or services operate independently of each other.

Fees or charges for goods or services may often be combined as part of the contract. This may well be the case where payment of the fee entitles the customer to purchase goods or services at lower prices than would otherwise be payable. In these circumstances the seller should recognize the fee on a systematic basis over the average period in which goods or services are expected to be provided to the customer.

Before the seller provides goods or services, it should report a credit (a liability) for the fee in the B/S to the extent that this has not been included in revenue. Where it can be demonstrated that the seller has no further obligations to the customer in respect of the fee, the seller should record the fee as turnover on the date on which it becomes entitled to it. This can be the case, for example, where, notwithstanding payment of the fee, the customer is required to pay all goods or services supplied under the arrangement at the current commercial rate.

An example may include recruitment agency services (success basis) – no revenue is generally recognized until the employment contract between the job seeker and the prospective employer is finalized as a result of the agent's services. As an example of revenue for these services on a success basis, the economic benefits associated with the transaction tend to flow to the organization until the significant action is completed (assuming there are no requirements for non-refundable deposits which would otherwise be recorded upfront as sales regardless of the final outcome).

Another example is a concert for which tickets are sold in advance. Perpetrators may be tempted to record the ticket fares at the time of receipts. However, revenue from artistic performance should be recognized when the event takes place. Similarly, for a course of ten monthly lessons when the tuition fee is paid in advance, perpetrators may record the fees at the time of receipts. However, revenue should be recognized over the period of the course – one-tenth per month.

In the construction industry, it is common to have long-term contracts which have a variety of contracted activities (so the sales revenues derive from these activities) falling into more than one financial year. As the activities fall into different financial years, determining the amount and timing of sales revenues (or profits) and the value of long-term contracts in B/S often become a controversial area. In fact, these involve a great deal of variations. In accordance with the matching principle, it has always been generally accepted that a prudently calculated 'attributable profit' be included in the P&L for the financial year in question.[10] However, attributable profit can be recognized only when the outcome of the contract can be assessed with reasonable certainty, and the profit so recognized should prudently reflect the amount of work performed to date. Inevitably, the recognition of attributable profits leaves a great deal of manoeuvre which may be abused by perpetrators. For example, the amount of attributable profit may be calculated by any of the three formulae:

- total estimated contract profit $\times \left(\dfrac{\text{value of work certified to date}}{\text{total contract price}} \right)$

- total estimated contract profit $\times \left(\dfrac{\text{cost of work completed}}{\text{estimated total costs}} \right)$

- total estimated contract profit $\times \left(\dfrac{\text{cash received}}{\text{total contract price}} \right)$

When the outcome of a construction contract can be estimated reliably, contract revenue and contract costs associated with the construction contract should be recognized as revenue and expenses respectively by reference to the stage of completion of the contract activity at the financial year-end.[11] However, each of the variables in the above formulae are vulnerable to abuses. Other than the assurance or representation from the organization's management, auditors may require adequate internal accounting and monitoring procedures in place to confirm the amount of profit recognized and to supply appropriate cost data to support the invoices.

CONCLUSION

Most businesses exist for the purpose of making a profit. The major contributor is sales. Accordingly, perpetrators have tried everything they can imagine to manipulate (usually to inflate) this key figure in the financial statements. The two main categories of overstatement of sales revenue are phantom sales and revocable sales. Sometimes, the dividing line is not clear.

Learning from experience, organizations should stay alert to warning signs of possible accounting irregularities in the overstatement of sales revenue. To end this chapter, various warning signs are set out for reference:

- abnormally high profit margin and possibly topping the industry as the fastest-growing organization;

- weak cash inflows from operations despite apparently healthy sales growth and profitability;

- significant transactions with related parties or other entities not in the ordinary course of business or where those entities are unaudited or audited by a different auditor;

- unusual or highly complex transactions whose substance and ownership is not known, especially those close to financial year-end, which might be examples of revocable sales;

- unexplained increase in the level of debtors and the debtor turnover days;

- unusual increase in sales recorded only in certain business units which are not shared by other parts of the same organization;

- gaps in sequence of important documents, such as customers' orders, dispatch notes, invoices and customers' payment remittance;

- missing originals of important documents, such as sales contracts, proof of customers' identities, customers' orders, dispatch notes, invoices and customers' payment remittance; and

- unusually high sales (or profit) targets, especially those set by investors after a change in ownership.

Notes

1, 3, 5, 6, 7, 8 – SSAP 18 *Revenue* (issued by the HKICPA in September 1995 and revised in January and May 2001, effective for accounting periods ending on or after 31 December 1995). The HKICPA is the successor to the Hong Kong Society of Accountants (HKSA).

2, 9 – FRS 5 *Substance of Transactions: Appendix G Reporting the Substance of Transactions: Revenue Recognition* (issued by the ASB in November 2003, effective for accounting periods ending on or after 23 December 2003). The ASB is the successor to the Accounting Steering Committee (ASC).

4, 5, 6, 8 – FRS 5 *Substance of Transactions* (issued by the ASB in April 1994 and amended in December 1994 and September 1998, effective for accounting periods ending on or after 22 September 1994).

10 – SSAP 9 *Stocks and Long-Term Contracts* (issued by the ASB in May 1975 and revised in September 1988, effective for accounting periods starting on or after 1 July 1988).

11 – SSAP 23 *Construction Contracts* (issued by the HKICPA in May 1998 and revised in January 2001, effective for accounting periods starting on or after 1 January 1998).

CHAPTER 4

Costing Less

UNDERSTATEMENT OF EXPENDITURE

'Costing less' is what drives some perpetrators. By understating the expenditure of an organization, perpetrators try to create a costing-less illusion – fabricating that the organization appears to have cost less than it has genuinely incurred in running its business. Defining the correct figures of costs or expenditure of an organization should be done with reference to the appropriate generally accepted accounting principles. Any departures from these are deemed to be irregular (accounting irregularities).

In an organization's profit and loss account, expenditure is the opposite of sales revenue. For any given level of sales revenue, an understatement of expenditure is translated into higher profits or lower losses. That is exactly the motive behind costing-less accounting irregularity. Costs, expenses, expenditure and losses (but not net losses) are similar terms and, if loosely defined, may be used interchangeably. This area of accounting irregularity involves suppressing and/or hiding expenditure or disguising its intent or purpose. It also covers any concealments or understatements of an obligation to pay because, under the accrual (or matching) concept (see Chapter 2), expenses are recorded as soon as they are incurred, regardless as to when the cash is spent.

RELEVANT GAAP IN HONG KONG AND THE UK

In Hong Kong, the first reference point for the accounting treatment of expenditure is the *Framework for the Preparation and Presentation of Financial Statements* (Framework) issued by the HKICPA in June 1997 (revised May 2003). The Framework basically defines expenditure as losses and expenses that arise in an organization's ordinary activities, such as cost of sales, wages, depreciation and other forms of outflow or depletion of assets such as cash, inventory, property, plant and equipment. Losses refer to other items that meet the definition of expenses and may, or may not, arise in an organization's ordinary activities. In essence, losses represent decreases in economic benefits and as such they are no different in nature from other expenses.

The recognition of expenses occurs together with an increase in liabilities or a decrease in assets. Accounting irregularities involving overstatement of assets and understatement of liabilities are considered in Chapters 5 and 6 respectively. With certain exceptions, expenses are generally recognized in the P&L on the basis of a direct association between the costs incurred and the earning of specific items of revenue – the accrual (or matching) concept. This matching process involves recognizing revenues and expenses of the same transactions or other events, such that various components of expense making up the cost of goods or services sold are recognized at the same time as the revenue derived from the sale of the goods or services. Certain exceptions may include advertising costs which are expensed as incurred even though the additional sales occur later. The determination is based on the strength and ease of measurement of the underlying association between the costs and the sales.

When economic benefits are expected to arise over several financial year-ends and the association with revenue is only loosely established, expenses are then recognized in the P&L on the basis of systematic and rational allocation procedures. This is often necessary in recognizing the expenses associated with the utilization of assets (such as properties and equipment); and this allocation of expenses is referred to as depreciation. These allocation procedures are intended to recognize expenses in the financial year in which the economic benefits associated with these items are utilized.

An expense is recognized immediately in the P&L when that item of expenditure produces no future economic benefits or when future economic benefits do not qualify, or cease to qualify, for recognition in the B/S as an asset. In some cases, an expense is recognized in the P&L when a liability is incurred without the recognition of an asset, such as the liability attached to a product warranty.

In the UK, the ASB issued *Statement of Principles for Financial Reporting* in December 1999 (Principles). Losses are defined as a decrease in ownership interest not resulting from distribution to owners and incorporates all forms of expenses, sometimes referred to as revenue expenditure as well as all recognized losses (realized and unrealized) on non-revenue items. The Principles also define ownership interest as the residual amount found by deducting all of the organization's liabilities (obligations to give economic benefits) from all of the organization's assets (rights to future economic benefits).

Expenditure of an organization may be visualized along a timescale as set out in Figure 4.1. Let us assume that the correct expenditure of the organization in question is $20 million for each of the three years (2004, 2005 and 2006) on the basis of appropriate GAAP. This gives a total of $60 million for the three years combined. To distort the total figure of $60 million and/or its allocation amongst the three years, in general, perpetrators may fabricate three types of accounting irregularities.

Firstly, off-book expenditure refers to the diversion of genuine expenses away from

Figure 4.1   Expenditure timescale

the organization in question. That means the reported annual expenditure of $20 million should have been higher, say $25 million. If the genuine expenditure incurred in 2004 is $25 million, of which $5 million is not recorded in the organization's books (off-book), the reported expenditure of $20 million is understated by $5 million.

Secondly, aggressive capitalization of expenditure refers to the shifting of the whole or partial amount of the $20 million of 2004 to 2005 and/or 2006 (to future financial years). The combined total for the three years is unchanged at $60 million.

The last category is lax policy in charging expenses, which has a similar effect to aggressive capitalization of expenditure. For those goods or services received by the organization in 2004, some are not invoiced by the vendors, say $1 million. Perpetrators may try to delay the unavoidable by not expensing the $1 million costs in 2004. The expenses (or the liabilities) are bound to surface in future periods (most possibly in 2005 when the invoice is issued and a payment is demanded).

ACCOUNTING IRREGULARITIES

Accounting irregularities involving understatement of expenditure can therefore be categorized as follows:

- off-book expenditure

- aggressive capitalization of expenditure

- lax policy in charging expenses.

OFF-BOOK EXPENDITURE

Off-book expenditure means that certain genuine expenses are completely absent from the organization's accounts. Put simply, off-book expenditure refers to business expenses paid and booked outside the business. This kind of accounting irregularity is relatively rare because it involves outflows of cash which must be funded by perpetrators or some other channels other than the organization in question. For this reason, the costs and efforts involved can easily outweigh the perceived benefits derived from the accounting irregularity. In some cases, the off-book expenditure is temporary with a specific intent and is reversible in the subsequent financial years. For example, buying raw materials with the perpetrator's own funds and using them for production would boost the organization's productivity because the cost of sales is understated. This may portray a rosy picture to bankers or prospective investors, which is to be subsequently reversed (and the perpetrator reimbursed). Let us consider a relevant example.

CASE 4.1

EXPENSES VIA OWNER'S PRIVATE FUNDS

Mr P is the proprietor and director of a manufacturing company (P Ltd). Mr P overrides P Ltd's usual controls in its materials receiving function, and P Ltd receives a shipment of raw materials worth $200 000 for use in its ordinary manufacturing process. The purchase order is placed by Mr P himself who also directs the invoice to himself and pays for the shipment from his own fund (not via P Ltd's funds).

The vendor is perfectly innocent, and it is an adopted practice for the owner of private companies to pay for business expenses from their own fund for reimbursement at a later stage (probably via a current account between the organization and its owners). The vendor is not in a position to challenge whether the amount is in fact properly charged to P Ltd.

This accounting irregularity creates an illusion of higher profitability for P Ltd (but at Mr P's own costs) because raw materials worth $200 000 are not recognized as cost of sales.

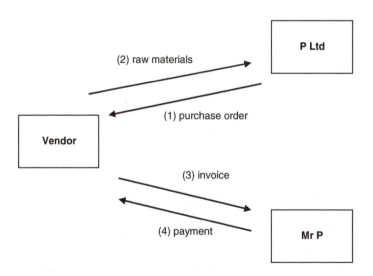

Figure 4.2   Expenses via owner's private funds

Stage 1 – Mr P's order to the vendor
Stage 2 – Delivery of raw materials to P Ltd
Stage 3 – Vendor's invoice to Mr P
Stage 4 – Payment of $200 000 from Mr P to the vendor

In essence, P Ltd benefits from the free use of $200 000 worth of raw materials which are financed by Mr P at his own costs. P Ltd's cost of sales is understated accordingly. A comparison of P Ltd's profit margins to the industry average shows a rather impressive picture (above-average profitability due to $200 000 worth of costs recorded off-book). To test the completeness of liabilities, audit confirmations are sent to all major suppliers, regardless of the size of their balances at the current financial year-end. Mr P is caught after an audit confirmation from the vendor in question reveals the discrepancy of the $200 000 shipment (in the vendor's book, the shipment is sold to P Ltd before the financial year-end and is subsequently settled by Mr P shortly after the financial year-end).

Following on from Case 4.1, transactions with related parties are most vulnerable to off-book expenditure accounting irregularities because the price and terms of related party transactions may well be massaged to achieve the desired figures.

In the UK, the ASB issued FRS 8 *Related Party Disclosures* in October 1995 effective for accounting periods starting on or after 23 December 1995. In Hong Kong, the HKICPA issued SSAP 20 *Related Party Disclosures* in August 1997 effective for accounting periods starting on or after 1 October 1997.

Related party relationships in commerce and business are not unusual. Transactions are presumed to be undertaken on an arm's-length basis: that is, at a price and on terms which could have been achieved in a transaction with an external party, in which each side bargains knowledgeably and freely, unaffected by any relationship between them.[1] These assumptions may not be justified when a related party relationship exists because the requisite conditions for competitive, free-market dealings may not be present.

Even when terms are arm's length, the disclosure of material-related party transactions is still relevant to the readers of financial statements. Based on the information, the readers are able to determine the degree of vulnerability to manipulation of future transactions as a result of the nature of the relationship than they would be in transactions with an unrelated party.[2]

Related parties may enter into transactions of a type that independent parties would not undertake or on terms that are unusually beneficial to the other parties. Where the effect of such transactions is material to an understanding of the financial statements, it will be necessary to give sufficient information about related party relationships and their transactions in order to ensure transparency in the financial statement disclosures.[3]

SSAP 20 of the HKICPA requires the disclosure of material transactions undertaken by the organization with related parties, irrespective of whether a price is charged. The objective is to ensure that financial statements contain the disclosures necessary to draw attention to the possibility that the reported financial positions and results may have been affected by material transactions with related parties.

Two or more parties are defined as related parties when:[4]

- one party has direct or indirect control of the other party;
- the parties are subject to common control from the same source;
- one party has influence over the financial operating policies of the other party to an extent that the other party might be inhibited from pursuing at all times its own separate interests; or
- the parties, in entering a transaction, are subject to influence from the same source to such an extent that one of the parties to the transaction has subordinated its own separate interests.

A related party transaction refers to a transfer of resources or obligations between related parties, regardless of whether a price is charged.[5] In essence, it means the transfer of assets or liabilities or the performance of services by, to or for a related party irrespective of whether a price is charged.[6]

If there are any transactions between related parties, the following disclosures should be made:[7]

- the nature of the related party relationships;
- the types of transactions; and
- the elements of the transactions necessary for an understanding of the financial statements.

The mere existence of a related party relationship may be sufficient to affect the transactions of the organization with other parties.[8] For example, a subsidiary may terminate relations with a trading partner following the acquisition by its parent of a fellow subsidiary engaged in the same trade as the former partner. Alternatively, a subsidiary may be refrained from continuing with its own activities due to instruction by its parent.

However, despite this potential impact on the results and financial position of the organization, SSAP 20 of the HKICPA takes the position that, because of the inherent difficulty in determining the effect of influences which do not lead to transactions, the disclosure of such relationships is not required. Therefore, unlike the International Accounting Standard and accounting practice in other regimes such as mainland China, SSAP 20 does not have a requirement to disclose related party relationships unless there have been transactions between the related parties.

International Accounting Standard IAS 24 *Related Party Disclosures* requires disclosure of related party relationships (where control exists) irrespective of whether there have been transactions between related parties. Except for the above difference, compliance with SSAP 20 of the HKICPA ensures compliance in all material respects with IAS 24.

Compliance with FRS 8 also ensures compliance with IAS 24 in all material respects except for the exemption in relation to certain subsidiaries. FRS 8 does not require disclosure in the financial statements of subsidiary undertakings (90 per cent or more of whose voting rights are controlled within the group) of transactions with organizations that are part of the group or investees of the group qualifying as related parties, provided that the consolidated financial statements in which that subsidiary is included are publicly available. IAS 24 does not require disclosure in the financial statements of a wholly owned subsidiary if its parent is incorporated in the same country and provides consolidated financial statements in that country.

Let us consider a relevant case.

CASE 4.2

DISCOUNTED PURCHASES AND A WEB OF RELATED PARTIES

A conglomerate of perpetrators (P Ltd) purchases regularly from various organizations. Some of the purchases are made at a heavy discount (below the market price). Accordingly, P Ltd enjoys an exceptionally good profit margin. However, P Ltd is caught by not disclosing details of the related party transactions which would otherwise alert the readers of P Ltd's financial statements against non-market transactions. Ultimately, P Ltd's costs are found to be understated by a significant sum as a result of the undercharged transactions with its related parties.

Not disclosing the related party transactions is irregular in the sense that the readers of the financial statements are not warned of the existence and nature of related party transactions. The mere existence of a related party relationship may be sufficient to affect the transactions of the organization with other parties.[9]

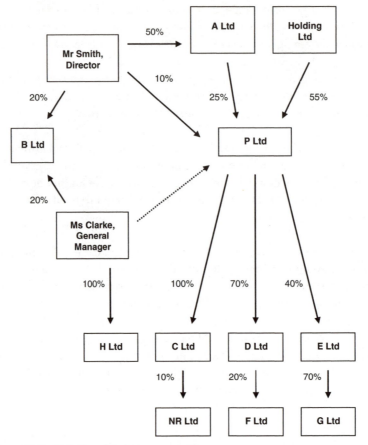

Figure 4.3   Relationship between parties

Other than NR Ltd, all organization (or individuals) in Figure 4.3 should be disclosed as related parties of P Ltd.

- A Ltd should be disclosed as a related party because it has significant influence over P Ltd.

- Mr Smith should be disclosed as a related party because he is a key management member (assuming he is an executive director involved in planning, directing or controlling the activities of P Ltd). However, it should be noted that Mr Smith's 50 per cent interest and hence significant influence in A Ltd alone is not conclusive in establishing a related party relationship with P Ltd. Mr Smith's 10 per cent interest in P Ltd alone is not conclusive in establishing a related party relationship with A Ltd since significant influence in P Ltd is not evidenced by the 10 per cent holding.

- Holding Ltd should be disclosed as a related party because it has control over P Ltd.

- B Ltd should be disclosed as a related party because either Mr Smith or Ms

> Clarke is able to exercise significant influence over B Ltd so that B Ltd and P Ltd are under common significant influence of either Mr Smith or Ms Clarke.
> - C Ltd and D Ltd should both be disclosed as related parties because P Ltd owns more than 50 per cent of each of them, indicating control rests with P Ltd.
> - E Ltd, a joint venture, should be disclosed as a related party because it is significantly influenced by P Ltd.
> - F Ltd should be disclosed as a related party because D Ltd could exercise significant influence over F Ltd, so that P Ltd has indirect control or significant influence over F Ltd.
> - G Ltd should be disclosed as a related party because it is a member of a group whose holding company is an associate of P Ltd. Ms Clarke should be disclosed as a related party if she constitutes a member of key management personnel – involved in planning, directing or controlling the activities of P Ltd.
> - H Ltd should be disclosed as a related party because it is owned and controlled by Ms Clarke, a key management member of P Ltd.

AGGRESSIVE CAPITALIZATION OF EXPENSES

Aggressive capitalization of expenses effectively means 'making an expense become an asset'. In the UK, the Companies Act 1985 allows the inclusion in the cost of production of an asset of:

- a reasonable proportion of the costs incurred by the company which are only indirectly attributable to the production of that asset; and

- interest on capital borrowed to finance the production of that asset, to the extent that it accrues in respect of the period of production.

In general, when costs cannot be related to any future economic benefits, amounts incurred should be charged to the P&L of the current financial year. Capitalization of expenses is to report an expenditure (including the actual spending and the accrued amount) as an asset rather than to expensing it and charging it to the current P&L. Therefore, taking an aggressive stand in capitalizing expenses is equivalent to an under-statement of expenditure (for the current period) – making an expense become an asset.

Expenses mean outflows or depletions of assets.[10] Capitalizing expenses as assets involves various aspects in accounting and GAAP, such as:

- Interest charges on borrowed funds and the appropriate accounting treatment is determined primarily on the basis of:
  - SSAP 19 *Borrowing Costs* (issued by the HKICPA in May 1996 effective for accounting periods starting on or after 1 April 1996);
  - FRS 15 *Tangible Fixed Assets* (issued by the ASB in February 1999, effective for accounting periods starting on or after 23 March 2000);

  – FRS 4 *Capital Instruments* (issued by the ASB in December 1993, effective for accounting periods ending on or after 22 June 1994).

- Items held for sale in the ordinary course of business and the appropriate accounting treatment is determined primarily on the basis of:
  – SSAP 22 *Inventory* (issued by the HKICPA in May 1998, revised January 2001, effective for accounting periods starting on or after 1 January 1998);
  – SSAP 9 *Stocks and Long-term Contracts* (issued by the ASB in May 1975, revised August 1980 and September 1988, effective for accounting periods starting on or after 1 July 1988).

- Assets in physical, tangible form and the appropriate accounting treatment is determined primarily on the basis of:
  – SSAP 17 *Property, Plant & Equipment* (issued by the HKICPA in July 1995, revised April 2001, effective for accounting periods starting on or after 1 January 2001);
  – FRS 15 *Tangible Fixed Assets* (issued by the ASB in February 1999, effective for accounting periods starting on or after 23 March 2000).

- Assets in intangible form and the appropriate accounting treatment is determined primarily on the basis of:
  – SSAP 29 *Intangible Assets* (issued by the HKICPA in January 2001, effective for accounting periods starting on or after 1 January 2001);
  – FRS 10 *Goodwill and Intangible Assets* (issued by the ASB in December 1997, effective for accounting periods ending on or after 23 December 1998);
  – SSAP 13 *Accounting for Research and Development* (issued by the ASB in December 1977, revised January 1989, effective for accounting periods starting on or after 1 January 1989).

A detailed examination of the above standards would go beyond the scope of this book, and readers are encouraged to refer to the original texts for a more advanced study of various subjects. Chapter 5 will involve some detailed discussions of accounting irregularities in overstating assets which are closely related to the understatement of expenditure and to some of the above standards.

Let us consider the appropriate GAAP relating to each of the above aspects and review certain aggressive attempts in understating the current financial year's expenses (which tend to simultaneously inflate the organization's assets at the current financial year-end).

Interest charges on borrowed funds

Borrowing costs are defined as interest and other costs incurred by an organization in connection with the borrowing of funds (such as finance charges, exchange differences, and amortization of ancillary costs and discounts or premiums relating to borrowings).[11]

When an organization borrows money in building an asset, rather than expensing the cost of borrowing in the current P&L, it may form part of the overall cost of that asset. A qualifying asset takes a substantial period of time to complete for its intended purpose, such as: manufacturing plant, power generation facilities, investment properties and inventories that turn into a saleable condition over a substantial period of time.

On the other hand, inventories that are routinely produced in large quantities on a repetitive basis and assets that are readily available for their intended use or sale when acquired are normally excluded. An organization may capitalize directly attributable finance costs as part of the cost of that asset.[12]

Finance cost may be defined as the difference between the net proceeds of a financial instrument (such as a debenture) and the total amount of the payments that the issuer (such as the borrower) may be required to make in respect of the instrument.[13] Directly attributable finance costs, in relation to the construction of a tangible fixed asset, are those that would have been avoided if there had been no expenditure on the asset. If finance costs are capitalized, capitalization should start when:

- finance costs are being incurred;
- expenditure on the asset is being incurred; and
- activities necessary to get the asset ready for use are in progress.

Capitalization of finance costs should cease when the asset is ready for use.

SSAP 19 of the HKICPA is based on IAS 23 (revised 1993) *Borrowing Costs*. There are no significant differences between the two accounting standards. In relation to interest charges on borrowed funds, the requirements of FRS 4 and FRS 15 in the UK are consistent with IAS 16 (revised 1998) *Property, Plant and Equipment* and IAS 23.

Items for sale

Inventories refer to assets which are:[14]

- held for sale in the ordinary course of business;
- in the process of production for such sale; or

- in the form of materials or supplies to be consumed in the production process or in the rendering of services.

The term 'inventories' is equivalent to 'stocks' used in SSAP 9 of the ASB as goods purchased for resale, consumable stores, materials purchased for incorporation into products for sale, products and services in intermediate stages of completion, and finished goods.

There are three components of the cost of inventories which are cost of purchase, cost of conversion and other costs incurred in bringing the inventories to their present location and condition.[15]

Costs of purchase comprise:

- purchase price (excluding trade discounts, rebates and subsidies);
- import duties and other irrecoverable taxes;
- inwards transportation and handling costs; and
- any other directly attributable costs.

Cost of conversion relates to the production process and includes direct labour and direct materials. It also includes a systematic allocation of fixed and variable production overheads that are incurred in converting materials into finished goods. Other costs may include non-production overheads or the costs of designing products for specific customers in the cost of inventories.

Compliance with SSAP 22 of the HKICPA or SSAP 9 of the ASB ensures compliance with IAS 2 *Inventories* in all material respects. The only substantial difference is that IAS 2 allows the LIFO (last-in-first-out) method to be adopted for the valuation of inventory, so long as certain additional disclosures are provided. Neither SSAP 22 of the HKICPA nor SSAP 9 of the ASB strictly prohibits the use of LIFO, but they both make clear that it is rarely going to be an appropriate method to use.

Let us consider a case of accounting irregularities involving the cost of inventories.

CASE 4.3

IRREGULAR CAPITALIZATION OF INVENTORIES

For the year 2004, a car manufacturer (P Ltd) achieves a gross profit of $24 million on $200 million of sales. Inventories and net profit are recorded at $45 million and $13 million respectively. P Ltd absorbs (capitalizes) the following costs in its inventories:

- invoice cost of metal used in casting frame
- invoice cost of engines imported from Germany
- import duties on the engines
- volume discounts received from the suppliers
- cost of scraps left over from moulds after casting
- wages of assembly-line workers
- wages of assembly-line maintenance personnel
- wages of security guard at the goods entrance gate
- advertising for assembly-line vacancies.

During the last quarter of 2004, P Ltd starts piling up inventories because a surge in consumer demands is anticipated. Meanwhile, P Ltd attempts to capitalize as much as possible into the inventories in order to suppress the recorded amount of costs of sales and operating costs in the P&L. P Ltd is caught when some items in the costs of inventories are found to be irregular:

- Exchange differences on subsequent payments for engines – which are irregular and should have been charged to the P&L.[16,17]

- Cost of scraps from castings due to incorrect moulds – which are abnormal amounts of wasted materials and labour. Only the cost of normal scrapping and wastage can be included in the cost of inventories.

- Wages of security guard at the goods exit gate and sales office cleaners – which should have been charged to the P&L as part of selling costs.

- Interest on bank overdraft – which is irregular because only borrowing costs specific to qualifying assets can be capitalized.

- Shipping costs of depot sales to foreign customers – which are the transportation of those cars that have been sold to customers. Only the cost of getting the inventories to their present location can be included in production overheads.

Table 4.1   Impact of accounting irregularities on P Ltd's financial statements

Extracts from P&L for 2004	Initial amounts (irregular) $ million	Adjusted amounts (regular) $ million
Turnover	200	200
Costs of sales	(176)	(180)
Gross profit	24	20
Other expenses	(11)	(12)
Net profit	13	8

Extracts from B/S as at 31 December 2004

	Initial amounts (irregular) $ million	Adjusted amounts (regular) $ million
Inventories	45	40
Net profit for the year	13	8

Costs of sales and other expenses are understated by $4 million (= $180m – $176m) and $1 million (= $12m – $11m) respectively as a result of the above accounting irregularities. This gives a total understatement of $5 million which are hidden (capitalized) in the carrying amount of the inventories. Both the inventories and profits are overstated by $5 million. In essence, $5 million of expenses in 2004 are brought forward to future years in the form of inflated inventories.

Assets in physical, tangible form

Tangible assets (tangible fixed assets) primarily include property, plant and equipment and are defined as those which:[18]

- are held by an organization for use in the production or supply of goods or services, for rental to others, or for administrative purposes; and

- are expected to be used during more than one financial year.

In the UK, FRS 15 of the ASB does not have a definition of tangible fixed assets. However, the Companies Act 1985 in the UK defines a fixed asset as one intended for use on a continuing basis in the company's activities, that is, it is not intended for resale.

An item of property, plant and equipment which qualifies for recognition as an asset or a tangible fixed asset should initially be measured at its cost.[19] The cost of an asset generally comprises:

- acquisition costs (including import duties and irrecoverable purchase taxes but excluding trade discounts and rebates); and

- directly attributable costs, such as site preparation, delivery and handling costs, installation costs and professional fees, and the estimated cost of dismantling and removing the asset and restoring the site (to the extent that it is recognized as a provision under SSAP 28 of the HKICPA or FRS 12 of the ASB – see Chapter 6).

Start-up costs, administrative expenses and general overheads do not form part of the cost of an asset unless they are necessary to bring the asset to its working condition. Capitalization of directly attributable costs should cease when the tangible fixed asset is ready for use (physically constructed), even if the asset has not really been brought into use.

After an item of property, plant and equipment has been recognized, an organization may incur additional expenditure. There are very limited circumstances in which further costs may be treated as part of the asset and not as an expense. Subsequent expenditure relating to an item of property, plant and equipment that has already been recognized should be added to the carrying amount of the asset when it is probable that future economic benefits, in excess of the originally assessed standard of performance of the existing asset, will flow to the organization.[20] All other subsequent expenditure should be recognized as an expense in the financial year in which it is incurred.

Therefore, the critical question is whether there are improvements which result in increased future economic benefits, such as:

- modification of an item of plant to extend its useful life, including an increase in its capacity;

- upgrading machine parts to achieve a substantial improvement in the quality of output; and

- adoption of new production processes enabling a substantial reduction in previously assessed operating costs.

The issue of subsequent expenditure concerns the distinction between revenue nature and capital nature.[21] Subsequent expenditure which ensures that a tangible fixed asset maintains its previously assessed standard of performance (such as repairs and maintenance expenses) is revenue expenditure and should be charged to the P&L. If this revenue expenditure is not incurred, then the previously estimated useful life may be shortened and the residual value of the tangible fixed asset reduced. This would result in extra depreciation which would also be charged to the P&L. Examples of this type of expenditure are servicing of machinery and painting of premises.

For subsequent expenditure in capital nature, examples are:

- where the expenditure enhances the economic benefits beyond those previously assessed;

- where a machine is upgraded by fitting improved parts (for example if a 2000 cc vehicle engine is replaced with a 3000 cc engine to enhance the use of the machine and/or to extend the economic useful life of the machine); and

- where the separate components of a tangible fixed asset are being separately depreciated, and one of those parts is replaced (for example where the roof, lift and central heating of a building are depreciated separately from the building itself. If one of these items was replaced, then any carrying amount of the old asset would be written off and the new expenditure capitalized).

The effect of accounting irregularities in this area is similar to those relating to inventories as discussed earlier. However, for inventories, the impact will be neutralized as soon as the inventories are sold off, which is likely to take place within the next financial year. For tangible fixed assets, the understatement of expenditure in the current P&L (due to aggressive capitalization of expenditure) is shifted to a longer period of time as and when the assets in question are being depreciated.

Let us consider a relevant case.

CASE 4.4

DATABASE SUBSCRIPTION

P Ltd provides a range of business consulting and investigating services and requires access to various companies and intelligence data in dealing with clients' issues. P Ltd subscribes for 12-month online access to a business intelligence database at $75 000. Rather than treating the costs as expenses, P Ltd capitalizes it as a fixed asset.

However, the nature and contents of this 12-month period of access to a business intelligence and search database is time sensitive, and its useful economic life to P Ltd is restricted to the 12-month period. Therefore, the correct treatment is to charge the entire sum to the P&L as the expenses are incurred. The impact of this accounting irregularity is that P Ltd's fixed assets (at cost) and net profit are both overstated by $75 000.

Assets in intangible form

Examples of assets in intangible form include scientific or technical knowledge, design and implementation of new processes or systems, computer software, patents, trademarks, copyrights, motion picture films, customer lists, mortgage servicing rights, fishing licences, import quotas, franchises, customer or supplier relationships, customer loyalty, market share and marketing rights.

SSAP 29 of the HKICPA defines an intangible asset as an identifiable non-monetary asset without physical substance held for use in the production or supply of goods or services, for rental to others, or for administrative purposes. If an item meets this definition of an intangible asset, expenditure to acquire (or generate it internally) forms part of the cost of an intangible asset. If the item is acquired in a business combination (an acquisition), it forms part of the goodwill recognized at the date of acquisition. Goodwill arising on a business combination represents a payment made by the buyer in anticipation of future economic benefits.

The definition of an intangible asset requires that an intangible asset be identifiable to distinguish it clearly from goodwill. The identifiability of an asset can commonly be demonstrated if the asset is separable, such that the organization could rent, sell, exchange or distribute the specific future economic benefits attributable to the asset without also disposing of future economic benefits that flow from other assets used in the same revenue-earning activity. For example, a pharmaceutical organization can sell a few of its research and development projects without disposing of its entire business.

An asset is a resource controlled by an organization as a result of past events and from which future economic benefits are expected to flow to the organization which is consistent with the definition in the Framework. To pass the test of controlling an asset, it is necessary that the organization has the power to obtain the future economic benefits flowing from the underlying resource and also can restrict the access of others to those benefits.

For tangible assets it would normally not be an issue to exercise the power to obtain the future economic benefits flowing from the underlying resource and to restrict access of others to those benefits. For intangible assets, the capacity of an organization to control the future economic benefits would normally be derived from legal rights that are enforceable in a court of law (for example, a brand name is protected by a trademark, a publishing title by copyright, a licence by contract). Market and technical knowledge may give rise to future economic benefits. For example, an organization may control those benefits if the knowledge is protected by legal rights such as copyrights, a restraint of trade agreement (where permitted) or by a legal duty to maintain confidentiality.

In the absence of legal rights, it is more difficult to demonstrate control over an intangible asset. For example, an organization may have a portfolio of customers or a market share and expects that, due to its efforts in building customer relationships and loyalty, the customers will continue to trade with the organization. However, in the absence of legal rights to protect, or other ways to control, the relationships with customers or the loyalty of the customers to the organization, the organization usually has insufficient control over the economic benefits from customer relationships and loyalty to consider that such items (portfolio of customers, market shares, customer relationships, customer loyalty) meet the definition of intangible assets.

The future economic benefits flowing from an intangible asset may include revenue from the sale of products or services, cost savings, or other benefits resulting from the use of the asset by the organization.

As for intangible assets, since their future economic benefits are consumed over time, the carrying amount of the asset is reduced to reflect that consumption by amortization. SSAP 29 of the HKICPA defines amortization as the systematic allocation of the depreciable amount of an asset over its estimated useful life.

In the UK, FRS 10 shares a very similar standing on the recognition of intangible assets and the capitalization of related costs.

Let us consider a case involving intangible assets.

CASE 4.5

IRREGULAR RECOGNITION OF INTANGIBLES

P-Global is an international chain of restaurants specializing in hamburgers and fried chicken. In 2000, P-Global grants an exclusive franchise to a company of perpetrators (P-HK) who pay a franchise fee for the use of the brand name of 'Super Burger' for the operation of three restaurant outlets in Hong Kong.

In 2001, P-HK starts to employ resources in developing a new series of its own brand name of Chinese nutritious food products, after carrying out a range of market surveys and feasibility studies. In 2003, the development process is completed and the prototypes of the nutritious food products are successfully tested and well received in a market survey, which also indicates that the series of food products would secure definite sales and profitability to P-HK. In 2004, P-HK opens its first restaurant selling the nutritious food products under its own registered brand name of 'Healthy Diet'.

P-HK incurs substantial expenditure for both the franchised business and the new brand-name nutritious food business and is in a tight financial position. P-HK capitalizes as many items as possible, including the following expenditure:

- the cost of computer software to operate the production plant, forming part of the property, plant and equipment;[21]

- franchise fees paid to P-Global for the use of Super Burger for the operation of the three outlets, as they are a directly attributable expenditure on separate acquisition of the rights to use Super Burger;

- a market survey on the quality of Healthy Diet's series of nutritious food, because the cost of testing the prototypes should form part of the development phase;[22]

- consultancy fees incurred for the development of Healthy Diet's series of nutritious food, because these are a directly attributed expenditure[23] to the extent that it was incurred after the development of Healthy Diet had met recognition criteria as an intangible asset;

- salary costs incurred for the development of Healthy Diet's nutritious food series, because wages and salaries qualify as an intangible asset to the extent that it was incurred after the development of Healthy Diet had met recognition criteria as an intangible asset; and

- interest on bank borrowings to finance the development of Healthy Diet's nutritious food series, because borrowing costs can be capitalized if the intangible asset qualifies as a qualifying asset to the extent that it is incurred after the development of Healthy Diet has met recognition criteria as an intangible asset.[24]

However, P-HK is under pressure to deliver a good business performance and pushes hard to minimize the recorded amounts of expenditure in the P&L. P-HK is caught with the following accounting irregularities:

- Formation costs for setting up new outlets of Super Burger and Healthy Diet (including legal fees for completing the required contracts, licences and registrations) – capitalization of the formation costs for the new outlets is irregular because start-up costs should be recognized as an expense unless it can be specifically included in the cost of an item of property, plant and equipment.[25]

- Staff training costs employed in new outlets – expenditure incurred on training activities should be recognized as an expense.[26]

- Advertising costs incurred prior to opening of the new outlets – expenditure incurred on advertising activities should be treated as an expense.[27]

- Relocation costs of an outlet after the lapse of an operating lease – expenditure incurred on relocating activities should be treated as an expense.[28]

- Costs incurred for the establishment and promotion of Healthy Diet – it is irregular because internally generated brands are prohibited from recognition.[29]

- A market survey consumer demand for Chinese nutritious food – it is irregular because expenditure incurred on general research activities should be recognized as an expense.[30]

- A share of the general overheads of research and development (rent, depreciation, and so on) as an allocation to the above development process – although the research and development overheads can be capitalized to the extent that they are necessary to generate the development activities and can be allocated on a reasonable and consistent basis to the products, general overheads allocated should be excluded.[31]

- A share of administrative overheads, as an allocation to the above development process – general administrative overheads cannot be allocated to intangible assets since they cannot be directly attributed to the development of the products.[32]
- Operating losses sustained in the Chinese nutritious food restaurant operation as they fall short of the planned performance for the first two quarters of the year – initial operating losses incurred before an asset achieves planned performance are not components of intangible assets.[33]

In many industries, such as those producing foods, medicines or high-technology products, the expenditure on research and development (R&D) is considerable. When R&D is a large item of cost, its accounting treatment may have a significant influence on the P&L and the B/S.

Research is defined as the original and planned investigation undertaken with the prospect of gaining new scientific or technical knowledge and understanding.[34] In the research phase of a project, it is not possible to demonstrate that a separately identifiable intangible asset exists that will generate probable future economic benefits. It can be divided into:

- basic (or pure) research which is experimental or theoretical work with no commercial end in view and no practical application;

- applied research which is original investigation directed towards a specific practical objective.

Both types of research expenditure should be charged to P&L as incurred.

On the other hand, development is defined as the application of research findings or other knowledge to a plan or design for the production of new or substantially improved materials, devices, products, processes, systems or services prior to the commencement of commercial production or use. Development is also the use of scientific or technical knowledge in order to produce new or substantially improved materials, devices, processes, and so on.[35]

Therefore, an organization can, in some instances, identify an intangible asset and demonstrate that the asset will probably generate future economic benefits. SSAP 29 of the HKICPA requires that an intangible asset arising from development should be recognized if, and only if, an organization can demonstrate *all* of the following:

- the technical feasibility of completing the intangible asset so that it will be available for use or sale;

- its intention to complete the intangible asset and use or sell it;

- its ability to use or sell the intangible asset;

- the way that the intangible asset will generate probable future economic benefits;

- the availability of adequate technical, financial and other resources to complete the development and to use or sell the intangible asset;

- its ability to reliably measure the expenditure attributable to the intangible asset during its development.

Expenditure on pure and applied research should be written off as incurred.[36] Development expenditure should be written off in the current financial year, except in certain circumstances when it may be deferred to future years provided six conditions are met:

- There is a separately defined project.

- The expenditure is separately identifiable.

- The project's outcome has been assessed with reasonable certainty as to:
  – its technical feasibility, and
  – its ultimate commercial viability.

- The aggregate of the deferred development costs, any further development costs, and related production, selling and administration costs is reasonably expected to be exceeded by related future sales or other revenues.

- Overall profit is expected from the project.

- Adequate resources exist to enable the project to complete.

LAX POLICY IN CHARGING EXPENSES

As previously discussed, in general, when costs cannot be related to any future economic benefits, amounts incurred should be charged to the P&L of the current financial year. As the expensing of certain costs is pushed to years other than the ones in which they actually occur, they are not properly matched against the revenue that they help to produce. In essence, revenue is recognized on the sale of certain items, but the cost of goods or services that go into the items sold are not recorded (intentionally) until the subsequent period. This effectively makes the entire amount of sales revenue from the transaction (without the deduction of the relevant costs) as profits. In the next year, profits would be depressed by the same amount.

Some accounting irregularities involve treating expenses incurred for the current financial year as prepayment rather than being charged to the current P&L. This results in an understatement in expenses and a corresponding overstatement in prepayment (assets).

Let us consider a relevant case.

CASE 4.6

DURATION OF A MAINTENANCE CONTRACT

On 1 January 2003, a company of perpetrators (P Ltd) pays $180 000 to a vendor (Vendor X) for an 18-month maintenance contract of its entire fleet of vehicles. P Ltd has a financial year-end of 31 December, and there is an 18-month contract from 1 January 2003 to 30 June 2004 which requires payment in advance. That means the maintenance expenses should be recorded at $10 000 a month. However, P Ltd gives a 'commission' of $2000 to Vendor X to alter the terms to a 24-month contract and agrees to sell its entire fleet and not to call any services during the six months from 1 July 2004 to 31 December 2004.

During the year-ended 31 December 2003, maintenance expense is incorrectly stated at $90 000; $120 000 is the correct amount of maintenance expenses. Therefore, at 31 December 2003, the expense is understated by $30 000 (= $90 000 – $120 000), and the prepayment is overstated by the same amount.

The loss to P Ltd is the bribe of $2000 to Vendor X, in return for an expense understatement of $30 000.

Expenses are charged to the current P&L because they are incurred by an organization during that period. Alternatively, there are costs which have been capitalized in a previous financial year and are now being released and allocated over several years in a systematic manner.

In some cases, lax policy in charging expenses may be fabricated via a misclassification of accounts in the financial statements. By classifying assets in a different (but irregular) way, perpetrators try to postpone the charging of certain expenditure to the P&L until some future years.

Let us consider a case involving property developers and property investors.

CASE 4.7

MISCLASSIFICATION BY PROPERTY DEVELOPERS

P Ltd is a property development group which relies upon selling the buildings they develop. Unlike property investors which are adequately financed until the sale of the property, P Ltd usually needs to sell, even if a building is tenanted. Indeed, some property developers cannot even cover their loan interest without regular disposals of buildings.

Therefore, P Ltd's buildings are inventories to its business, and inventories should be stated in the B/S at the lower of cost or net realizable value. If the net realizable value of P Ltd's buildings falls below cost, P Ltd should write down the carrying value of inventories and show it as a charge (provision or write-off) in the P&L.

The same is of course not true for fixed assets. An item of property, plant and equipment which qualifies for recognition as an asset or a tangible fixed asset should initially be measured at its cost.[37] The cost of an asset generally comprises:

- acquisition costs (including import duties and irrecoverable purchase taxes but excluding trade discounts and rebates); and

- directly attributable costs, such as site preparation, delivery and handling costs, installation costs and professional fees, and the estimated cost of dismantling and removing the asset and restoring the site (to the extent that it is recognized as a provision under SSAP 28 of the HKICPA and FRS 12 of the ASB – see Chapter 6).

Fixed assets are generally not for trading. So instead of being valued at the lower of cost or market value, they are included in the B/S at historic cost less any depreciation. Sometimes property assets are subject to periodic revaluations. Even if the market value drops below the B/S value, fixed assets can still be stated at cost as long as the value in use (that is, the present value of the future cash flows obtained as a result of the organization's continued use of the asset) is above the cost. Therefore, the fall in the market value of fixed assets is not necessarily reflected in the P&L since they are not held for resale.

For P Ltd, there is a recession causing a sharp fall in the value of their inventories (buildings) below cost level. P Ltd takes advantage of the flexibility in accounting, and discovers that they may be able to get away with the resulting loss if they re-classify the assets from current assets to fixed assets. However, P Ltd's accounting treatment is questioned by the auditors and is subsequently reversed. Chapter 7 will deal with more accounting irregularities in the area of manipulation of classification and disclosures.

Another example of lax policy in charging expenses relate to the depreciation or amortization charges, or, more precisely, the calculation of these charges.

Following on from the earlier discussion about SSAP 17 of the HKICPA and FRS 15 of the ASB, depreciation is defined as the systematic allocation of the depreciable amount of an asset over its estimated useful life.[38] Depreciation is also defined as the measure of the cost or revalued amount of the economic benefits of the tangible fixed asset that has been consumed during the period.[39]

As the economic benefits embodied in an asset are consumed by the organization, the carrying amount of the asset is reduced to reflect this consumption, normally by charging depreciation to the P&L. The depreciable amount is the cost (or the fair value at the date of revaluation) of an asset as included in the balance sheet, less the asset's estimated residual value. The depreciable amount of a tangible asset should be allocated on a systematic basis over its useful economic life.

A variety of methods can be used to allocate the depreciable amount of a tangible fixed asset on a systematic basis over its useful economic life. We have already considered the components of the costs under SSAP 17 of the HKICPA and FRS 15 of the ASB. The residual value is the net amount that the organization expects to obtain for an asset at the end of its useful life after deducting the expected costs of disposal.

Therefore, a great deal of discretion is left to the organization in deciding on depreciation. The amount of deprecation charged to one period's P&L is dependent on four variables:

- the asset's depreciable amount (its costs)

- the asset's residual value

- the adopted depreciation or amortization method

- the asset's estimated useful life.

Similarly, for intangible assets, since their future economic benefits are consumed over time, the carrying amount of the asset is reduced to reflect that consumption by amortization. SSAP 29 of the HKICPA defines amortization in the same way as depreciation in SSAP 17, which is as the systematic allocation of the depreciable amount of an asset over its estimated useful life.

SSAP 29 of the HKICPA requires that:

- the depreciable amount of an intangible asset should be allocated on a systematic basis over the best estimate of its useful life (normally less than 20 years);

- amortization should commence when the asset is available for use.

The assessment of the useful life of an asset requires the exercise of judgement by management. In determining the useful life, which has a critical role to play in the amount of depreciation being expensed in the P&L from year to year, the following factors need to be considered:[40]

- the expected usage of the asset by the organization and whether the asset could be efficiently managed by another management team;

- typical product life cycles for the asset, and public information on estimates of useful lives of similar types of assets that are used in a similar way;

- technical, technological or other types of obsolescence;

- the stability of the industry in which the asset operates, and changes in the market demand for the products or services output from the asset;

- expected actions by competitors or potential competitors;

- the level of maintenance expenditure required to obtain the expected future economic benefits from the asset, and the company's ability and intent to reach such a level;

- the period of control over the asset, and legal or similar limits on the use of the asset, such as the expiry dates of related leases; and

- whether the useful life of the asset is dependent on the useful life of other assets of the organization.

In view of rapid technological changes, the useful life of computer software and many other intangible assets is likely to be short. If the useful life is set unrealistically long, the depreciation is expensed at an unjustifiably slow pace. Uncertainty justifies estimating the useful life of an intangible asset on a prudent basis, but it does not justify choosing a life that is unrealistically short (which means the depreciation to the P&L is accelerated).

The amortization method used should reflect the pattern in which the asset's economic benefits are consumed by the organization.[41] Intangible assets may be amortized by the same systematic and rational methods such as the straight-line method, the diminishing balance method and the unit of production method. However, SSAP 29 takes the view that it will rarely be the case that an amortization method that results in a lower amount of accumulated amortization than under the straight-line method can be justified.

The useful economic lives of goodwill and intangible assets should be reviewed at the end of each year.[42] If a life is changed then the carrying value should be amortized over the revised remaining life. If the review increases the life to more than 20 years from the date of the acquisition of the asset, then impairment reviews are necessary. Where they have indefinite lives, then they should not be amortized. Indefinite lives or periods longer than 20 years may be used.

The calculation of amortization requires that the residual value of an intangible asset should be assumed to be zero unless:[43]

- there is a commitment by a third party to purchase the asset at the end of its useful life; or

- there is an active market for the asset, and:
  - residual value can be determined by reference to that market, and
  - it is probable that such a market will exist at the end of the asset's useful life.

The cost and residual value (the depreciable amount) define the total amount to be depreciated or amortized. It is important to note that the total depreciable amount to the organization is the same regardless how the estimated useful economic life and the basis of depreciation method are determined. Any overstatements of the asset's estimated useful life will understate the depreciation or amortization charge of one given period's P&L. For existing fixed assets, changing the depreciation policy from the straight-line method to the reducing-balance method (but keeping the depreciation rate unchanged) may be an attempt to commit accounting irregularities. This is illustrated as follows:

CASE 4.8

USEFUL LIFE OF FIXED ASSETS

A company of perpetrators (P Ltd) buys a machine for $230 000 in 2004 and uses it in its factory's production. The machine is estimated to have a useful life of four years with a residual value of $30 000 at the end of its fourth year. P Ltd adopts the straight-line method to allocate the depreciable amount (depreciation calculation). The correct annual depreciation charge is therefore calculated as ((230 000 – 30 000)/4), as illustrated in Table 4.2.

However, P Ltd wants to boost its profits for 2004 to 2007 and takes an overly optimistic estimate of the useful economic life of the machine at five years. Therefore, expenses for 2004–2007 are understated by $10 000 per annum, while the total charges over the relevant periods (four and five years) remain the same at $200 000.

Table 4.2 Annual depreciation charge

	Correct figures	Irregular figures	Irregular figures
Estimated useful life	4 years	5 years	4 years
Residual value	$30 000	$30 000	$50 000
Year	Annual depreciation charge $	Annual depreciation charge $	Annual depreciation charge $
2004	50 000	40 000	45 000
2005	50 000	40 000	45 000
2006	50 000	40 000	45 000
2007	50 000	40 000	45 000
2008	0	40 000	0
Depreciable amount	200 000	200 000	180 000

Alternatively, P Ltd may try another way to massage the profit figure by overstating the residual value of the machine, say, inflating it from $30 000 to $50 000 (same useful life of four years). The expense for 2004–2007 is therefore understated by $5000 per annum; the depreciable amount is $20 000 less but this is offset by increase in loss (or decrease in gain) on disposal of the machine (though the gain or loss on disposal is likely to be shown as a non-recurring item).

Another problematic area of lax policy in charging expenses is on the provisions for doubtful debts. Liabilities and provisions are thoroughly discussed in Chapter 6. Very briefly, a provision is an obligation to pay or an expected reduction in the value of an asset but with a high degree of uncertainty in respect of the timing and amount of the outflow of resources.

For one reason or another, some customers are unable to pay for goods and services with which they have been provided. Although organizations take steps to minimize their bad and doubtful debts, this problem is inevitable. When sales are made on credit, there are risks of uncollectability over some trade debts. According to the accrual (matching) principle, these losses, as normal business expenses, should be matched with the sales revenue of the period in which transactions occurred, rather than in the period when the specific trade debtors are found to be doubtful and uncollectable.

There are specific write-offs of bad debts for losses arising from an uncollectable debt when it becomes apparent that the particular account is bad. There are also doubtful debts. It is difficult for an organization to know bad debts in advance; doubtful debts should be assessed in advance and the corresponding losses should be provided in the P&L as expenses.

Generally, there are two ways of estimating the expected uncollectable accounts which are deducted from the total outstanding trade debts. The net sales approach focuses the P&L figures to estimate uncollectable expenses. Provisions for doubtful debts can be estimated as a percentage of sales or credit sales. It emphasizes the expense side of the adjustment and does not consider the level of existing balance of the bad debt account.

The second approach, outstanding trade debts approach, focuses on the B/S. Provisions for doubtful debts expense can be estimated as a percentage of the outstanding debtors. It adjusts the trade debt account to a new balance equal to the estimated collectable position. The approach requires an ageing analysis of the outstanding trade debtors. The adjusting entry takes into consideration the existing balance of the trade debt accounts.

The net sales approach is theoretically sound because it matches the doubtful debt expenses against the revenues of the current period that caused the trade debt account (which is bad). Thus it focuses on matching current revenues with current expenses and emphasizes the P&L rather than the B/S. The use of credit sales rather than total sales (cash sales + credit sales) as the basis for adjustments is preferable because cash sales do not cause credit risks. However, the overall level of provision required may change from year to year in accordance with the business cycle, rather than the profile of the outstanding debts.

The outstanding trade debts approach suffers from the probability that doubtful debt expense reported on the P&L for the period may not be related to the credit sales of the current period, which violates the matching principle. It is often useful to combine the two approaches in particular, an ageing analysis of debtors can help to evaluate the profile of the debts at the end of each financial year, that is, the recoverable amount of debtors.

The attraction of the provision for doubtful debts to perpetrators is that it can affect the B/S and the P&L, and it can be changed from one year to another. In the year when carrying of receivables appears to be higher than required they can be reduced, and when the values are smaller than desired they can be increased. As the provision for doubtful debt is reflected in the P&L, it can also be used to smooth the reported profit so as to improve efficiency ratios.

Let us consider a relevant case.

CASE 4.9

CHANGE IN THE PROVISION FOR DOUBTFUL DEBTS

P Ltd has sales of $13 million in 2004 with outstanding debtors totalling $8 million at 31 December 2004 ($6 million at 31 December 2003). P Ltd's existing policy of provision for doubtful debts is on the basis of 3 per cent of the total outstanding debtors.

Despite a slowdown in the economy and an increase in the number of corporate failures (the credit risk is rising), the management of P Ltd tries to suppress the level of doubtful debts in order to maximize the reported profit in the P&L. Accordingly, P Ltd adopts a new policy of provision for doubtful debts on the basis of 1 per cent of total sales which is calculated at $130 000 (= $13 000 000 × 1%). P Ltd's auditors challenge this new policy and qualify this accounting irregularity in Table 4.3 below:

Table 4.3 P Ltd's doubtful debts

Extracts from financial statements	31 Dec 04	31 Dec 03
	$	$
Sales	13 000 000	n/a
Trade debtors	8 000 000	6 000 000
Existing policy (3% on debtors)		
Provision for doubtful debts		
$8 000 000 × 3%	240 000	180 000
Charge of doubtful debts in P&L	60 000	n/a
New policy (1% on sales)		
Provision for doubtful debts		
$13 000 000 × 1%	130 000	180 000
Credit of doubtful debts in P&L	(50 000)	n/a

Under the existing policy, P Ltd's provision for doubtful debts should be at $24 000 (= $8 000 000 × 3%). This gives a charge to the P&L at $60 000 (= $240 000 – $180 000). However, the new policy sets aside only $130 000 (= $13 000 000 × 1%) as provision which gives a credit to the P&L at $50 000 (= $130 000 – $180 000). Therefore, the charge of doubtful debts is understated by $110 000 (= $60 000 + $50 000) in total.

This issue is closely related to Chapters 5 and 6 where we will discuss the accounting irregularities involving overstatement of assets (Owning More) and understatement of liabilities (Owing Less).

CONCLUSION

Since expenditure is deducted from sales revenue in calculating profits, understating expenditure has the same impact on the profit figure as overstatement of sales revenue as already discussed in Chapter 3. The three main categories of understatement of expenditure are off-book expenditure, aggressive capitalization of expenses and lax policy in charging expenses. The dividing line is often not clear.

Learning from experience, organizations should stay alert to certain warning signs that indicate possible accounting irregularities in the understatement of expenditure. To end this chapter, various warning signs are set out for reference:

- exceptionally low cost structure compared to the scale of operations;

- continuously topping the industry as the cost leader, despite competition;

- unusually high profit targets or aggressive cost-saving plans, especially those set by investors after a change in ownership;

- achievement of aggressive cost-savings plans in comparison with high cash outflows from operations;

- significant transactions with related parties or other entities not in the ordinary course of business or where those entities are unaudited or audited by a different auditor;

- unusual or highly complex transactions whose substance and ownership is not known, especially those close to financial year-end;

- unexplained increase in the account payables and/or creditor turnover days;

- unusual increase in costs of sales recorded only in certain business units which are not shared by other parts of the same organization;

- gaps in the sequence of important documents, such as purchase orders, goods receipt notes, and suppliers' invoices and statements; and

- missing originals of important documents, such as purchase orders, goods receipt notes, and suppliers' invoices and statements.

Notes

1, 2, 4, 6, 7 – FRS 8 *Related Party Disclosures* (issued by the ASB in October 1995, effective for accounting periods starting on or after 23 December 1995). The ASB is the successor to the Accounting Standards Committee (ASC)

3, 4, 5, 7, 8, 9 – SSAP 20 *Related Party Disclosures* (issued by the HKICPA in August 1997, effective for accounting periods starting on or after 1 October 1997). The HKICPA is the successor to the Hong Kong Society of Accountants (HKSA)

10 – The HKICPA, *Framework for the Preparation and Presentation of Financial Statements*, issued in June 1997 and revised in May 2003
 – The ASB, *Statement of Principles for Financial Reporting*, issued in December 1999

11, 24 – SSAP 19 *Borrowing Costs* (issued by the HKICPA in May 1996, effective for accounting periods starting on or after 1 April 1996)

12, 19, 21, 37, 39 – FRS 15 *Tangible Fixed Assets* (issued by the ASB in February 1999, effective for accounting periods starting on or after 23 March 2000)

13 – FRS 4 *Capital Instruments* (issued by the ASB in December 1993, effective for accounting periods ending on or after 22 June 1994)

14, 15 – SSAP 22 *Inventory* (issued by the HKICPA in May 1998, revised January 2001, effective for accounting periods starting on or after 1 January 1998)

15 – SSAP 9 *Stocks and Long-term Contracts* (issued by the ASB in May 1975, revised August 1980 and September 1988, effective for accounting periods starting on or after 1 July 1988)

16 – SSAP 11 *Foreign Currency Translation* (issued by the HKICPA in February 1985, revised in July 1996 and December 2001, effective for accounting periods starting on or after 1 January 2002)

17 – SSAP 20 *Foreign Currency Translation* (issued by the ASB in April 1983, effective for accounting periods starting on or after 1 April 1983)

18, 19, 20, 21, 37, 38 – SSAP 17 *Property, Plant & Equipment* (issued by the HKSA, the predecessor of the HKICPA in July 1995, revised April 2001, effective for accounting periods starting on or after 1 January 2001)

18, 19, 20, 21, 37, 38 – FRS 15 *Tangible Fixed Assets* (issued by the ASB in February 1999, effective for accounting periods starting on or after 23 March 2000)

22, 23, 24, 34, 40, 41, 43 – SSAP 29 *Intangible Assets* (issued by the HKICPA in January 2001, effective for accounting periods starting on or after 1 January 2001)

25 – para 54c of SSAP 29 *Intangible Assets* (issued by the HKICPA in January 2001, effective for accounting periods starting on or after 1 January 2001)

26 – para 57b of SSAP 29 *Intangible Assets* (issued by the HKICPA in January 2001, effective for accounting periods starting on or after 1 January 2001)

27 – para 57c SSAP 29 *Intangible Assets* (issued by the HKICPA in January 2001, effective for accounting periods starting on or after 1 January 2001)

28 – para 57d SSAP 29 *Intangible Assets* (issued by the HKICPA in January 2001, effective for accounting periods starting on or after 1 January 2001)

29 – para 51 SSAP 29 *Intangible Assets* (issued by the HKICPA in January 2001, effective for accounting periods starting on or after 1 January 2001)

30 – para 44 SSAP 29 *Intangible Assets* (issued by the HKICPA in January 2001, effective for accounting periods starting on or after 1 January 2001)

31 – para 54b SSAP 29 *Intangible Assets* (issued by the HKICPA in January 2001, effective for accounting periods starting on or after 1 January 2001)

32 – para 55a SSAP 29 *Intangible Assets* (issued by the HKICPA in January 2001, effective for accounting periods starting on or after 1 January 2001)

33 – para 55b SSAP 29 *Intangible Assets* (issued by the HKICPA in January 2001, effective for accounting periods starting on or after 1 January 2001)

35, 36 – SSAP 13 *Accounting for Research and Development* (issued by the ASC/ASB in December 1977, revised January 1989, effective for accounting periods starting on or after 1 January 1989)

42 – FRS 10 *Goodwill and Intangible Assets* (issued by the ASB in December 1997, effective for accounting periods ending on or after 23 December 1998)

CHAPTER 5

Owning More

OVERSTATEMENT OF ASSETS

'Owning more' is what drives some perpetrators. By overstating the assets of an organization, perpetrators try to create the illusion that the organization appears to have more strengths and capabilities than it genuinely possesses. Defining the correct figures of an organization's assets should be done with reference to the appropriate generally accepted accounting principles. Any departures from these are deemed to be irregular (accounting irregularities).

Valuing a business can be approached in many different ways. In general, there are two main methodologies in business valuation – earning-based and asset-based. Earning-based methodology focuses on the earning ability and cash flows of an organization as reflected by its future stream of profits. The prime variable used in this methodology is the future cash flows of the organization in question. In the long run, an organization's net cash flow equates to its net profit figure (after tax) which in turn is dependent upon the two main components, sales revenue and expenditure, which have been considered in Chapters 3 and 4 respectively. The second methodology is asset based, which focuses on an organization's financial strengths and operating capabilities. Based on the reported value and quality of an organization's assets, the prime variable used in asset-based valuation methodology is an organization's net assets (total assets less total liabilities).

Business valuation issues often play a crucial role in organizations' decision-making. We have already considered accounting irregularities involving overstatement of sales revenues and understatement of expenditure. In this chapter, we look at overstatement of assets, and understatement of liabilities will be discussed in Chapter 6.

RELEVANT GAAP IN HONG KONG AND THE UK

In Hong Kong, the first reference point for the accounting treatment of assets is the *Framework for the Preparation and Presentation of Financial Statements* (Framework) issued by the HKICPA in June 1997 (revised May 2003). The Framework states that the future economic benefit embodied in an asset is the potential to contribute, directly or indirectly, to the flow of cash and cash equivalents to the organization.

In the UK, the ASB issued *Statement of Principles for Financial Reporting* in December 1999 (Principles). As one of the seven elements of financial statements, assets are defined as rights or other access to future economic benefits controlled by an organization as a result of past transactions or events.

An asset is recognized in the balance sheet (B/S) when it is probable that the future economic benefits will flow to the organization and the asset has a cost or value that can be measured reliably. An asset is recognized when expenditure has been incurred for which it is probable that economic benefits will flow to the organization beyond the current financial year. Otherwise, those transactions should be recognized as an expense in the profit and loss account (P&L).

There is a close but not absolute association between expenditure and assets. Incurring expenditure may indicate that future economic benefits are sought, although the item may not satisfy the definition of an asset. Similarly the absence of a related expenditure does not preclude an item from satisfying the definition of an asset. For example, a contribution from an organization's proprietor or a donation received by an organization is not an expense but satisfies the definition of an asset.

Many assets, such as property, plant and equipment, have a physical form. However, physical form is not essential to the existence of an asset and intangibles such as patents and copyrights are assets if future economic benefits are expected to flow from them to the organization and if they are controlled by the organization.

SSAP 29 *Intangible Assets* (issued by the HKICPA in January 2001, effective for accounting periods starting on or after 1 January 2001) defines an intangible asset as an identifiable non-monetary asset without physical substance held for use in the production or supply of goods or services, for rental to others, or for administrative purposes.

In the UK, the ASB issued FRS 10 *Goodwill and Intangible Assets* in December 1997, effective for accounting periods ending on or after 23 December 1998. Intangible assets are defined as non-financial fixed assets that do not have physical substance but are identifiable and are controlled by the organization through custody or legal rights.

Many other assets (for example, debtors and properties) are associated with legal rights, including the right of ownership. In determining the existence of an asset, however, the right of ownership is not essential. For example, property held on a lease is an asset if the organization controls the benefits which are expected to flow from the property. Although an organization's capacity to control benefits is usually derived from the legal rights, an item may still satisfy the definition of an asset even when there is no legal control. Know-how obtained from a development activity may meet the definition of an asset when, by keeping that know-how secret, an organization controls the benefits that are expected to flow from it.

In essence, an asset is a resource:[1]

- controlled by an organization as a result of past events; *and*
- from which future economic benefits are expected to flow to the organization.

An intangible asset should be recognized if, and only if:[2]

- it is probable that the future economic benefits that are attributable to the asset will flow to the organization; *and*
- the cost of the asset can be measured reliably.

The Principles state that rights or other access refers to the right to receive benefits rather than the asset itself or the legal ownership. This definition therefore requires certain leases to be capitalized even though the leased assets are not legally owned (SSAP 21 *Accounting for Leases and Hire Purchase Agreement*, issued by the ASB in August 1984, amended February 1997, effective for accounting periods starting on or after 1 July 1984 – see Chapter 6).

Future economic benefits make it clear that all assets must ultimately yield cash inflow into the organization. As financial statements are records of past transactions, an emphasis on past events in the definition of assets is important.

The accounting treatments of assets involve various aspects in accounting and GAAP, such as:

- Items held for sale in the ordinary course of business and the appropriate accounting treatment is determined primarily on the basis of:
  - SSAP 22 *Inventory* (issued by the HKICPA in May 1998, revised January 2001, effective for accounting periods starting on or after 1 January 1998)
  - SSAP 9 *Stocks and Long-term Contracts* (issued by the ASB in May 1975, revised August 1980 and September 1988, effective for accounting periods starting on or after 1 July 1988).
- Assets in physical, tangible form and the appropriate accounting treatment is determined primarily on the basis of:

> – SSAP 17 *Property, Plant & Equipment* (issued by the HKICPA in July 1995, revised April 2001, effective for accounting periods starting on or after 1 January 2001)
> – FRS 15 *Tangible Fixed Assets* (issued by the ASB in February 1999, effective for accounting periods starting on or after 23 March 2000).

- Assets in intangible form and the appropriate accounting treatment is determined primarily on the basis of:
  - SSAP 29 *Intangible Assets* (issued by the HKICPA in January 2001, effective for accounting periods starting on or after 1 January 2001)
  - FRS 10 *Goodwill and Intangible Assets* (issued by the ASB in December 1997, effective for accounting periods ending on or after 23 December 1998).

- Impairment of assets and the appropriate accounting treatment is determined primarily on the basis of:
  - SSAP 31 *Impairment of Assets* (issued by the HKICPA in January 2001, effective for accounting periods starting on or after 1 January 2001)
  - FRS 11 *Impairment of Fixed Assets and Goodwill* (issued by the ASB in July 1998, effective for accounting periods ending on or after 23 December 1998).

A detailed examination of the above standards would go beyond the scope of this book, and readers are encouraged to refer to the original texts for a more advanced study of these subjects. It is important to remember the basics of accounting irregularities and the double-entry book-keeping regime as introduced in Chapter 2. Expenses of the current financial year in the P&L are understated and carried forward to succeeding financial years to the extent that assets are overstated in the B/S. Chapters 3 and 4 include some discussions of accounting irregularities in overstating revenue and understating expenditure, which are closely related to the overstatement of assets and some of the above standards.

Let us consider the appropriate GAAP and review some aggressive attempts in inflating the assets in organizations' financial statements.

The sequence of our discussion in this chapter follows three categories of assets:

- tangible fixed assets

- inventories

- trade debtors.

TANGIBLE FIXED ASSETS

As discussed in Chapter 4, tangible fixed assets (tangible assets or fixed assets) primarily include property, plant and equipment and are defined as those which:[3]

- are held by an organization for use in the production or supply of goods or services, for rental to others, or for administrative purposes; *and*

- are expected to be used during more than one financial year.

In the UK, FRS 15 of the ASB does not have a definition of tangible fixed assets. However, the Companies Act 1985 in the UK defines a fixed asset as one intended for use on a continuing basis in the organization's activities, that is, it is not intended for resale.

An item of property, plant and equipment which qualifies for recognition as an asset or a tangible fixed asset should initially be measured at its cost.[4] The cost of an asset generally comprises:

- acquisition costs (including import duties and irrecoverable purchase taxes but excluding trade discounts and rebates); and

- directly attributable costs, such as site preparation, delivery and handling costs, installation costs and professional fees, and the estimated cost of dismantling and removing the asset and restoring the site (to the extent that it is recognized as a provision under SSAP 28 *Provisions, Contingent Liabilities and Contingent Assets* of the HKICPA or FRS 12 *Provisions, Contingent Liabilities and Contingent Assets* of the ASB – see Chapter 6).

Start-up costs, administrative expenses and general overheads do not necessarily form part of an asset's costs unless they are incurred in bringing the asset to its working condition. Capitalization of directly attributable costs should cease when the tangible fixed asset is ready for use (physically constructed), even if the asset has not actually been brought into use or met its target capacity.

Tangible fixed assets in the B/S are reported by two components – quantities and unit value, thus:

$$\text{Total value} = \text{Quantities} \times \text{Unit value}$$

Therefore, in overstating tangible fixed assets, perpetrators may manipulate either of the two components. There are at least three ways to do so:

- overstating physical count

- inflating unit value

- delaying depreciation or amortization.

OVERSTATING PHYSICAL COUNT OF TANGIBLE FIXED ASSETS

One of the accounting irregularities in overstating tangible fixed assets is to manipulate the physical count or to record fictitious quantities of tangible fixed assets.

If an organization's tangible fixed assets are located in many different sites, this kind of accounting irregularity can easily be overlooked. In addition, perpetrators may try shifting tangible fixed assets between different locations at or around the financial year-end. It often creates confusion as to which location the tangible fixed assets in transit should have been recorded and causes duplication in recording the tangible fixed assets. The problem is made more difficult to discover when tangible fixed assets at different locations are audited by different persons.

As part of the double-entry book-keeping regime, the corresponding entry of fictitious tangible fixed assets may be recorded as an amount payable to a vendor which is one of the perpetrator's accomplices. Alternatively, if the owner is also involved in the scheme (to cheat an external party such as the banker), it is common to use the capital account (or amount due to shareholders) representing an additional equity injection (or loan). That means the fictitious tangible fixed assets are contributed from the owner who would be able to confirm the additional equity injection. Accounting irregularity involving the owner would be more difficult to identify.

Another possible overstatement in physical count is to create fictitious title documents or purchase invoices to support the existence of certain tangible fixed assets which do not really exist. However, a physical verification check by the auditors is likely to reveal the deficiencies. In some cases, the tangible fixed asset in question may appear to be in existence during the physical verification check, but in fact it is not. For example, the make and model specification tag on an inferior (or scrapped) set of machinery may be manipulated to change it into what is recorded in the fixed-asset register. In addition, the complete fact and the status of ownership are not frankly disclosed, as the tangible fixed asset in question could have been leased, not owned outright.

Let us consider a relevant case.

CASE 5.1

OWNING MORE THAN NECESSARY

Mr P anticipates a bid from an institutional investor for his design business, Design P. Mr P tries many aggressive ways to portray Design P as a substantial business with a strong backing of assets, which include a fabricated injection of ten sets of the latest computers together with state-of-the-art graphic design peripherals.

As an injection by Mr P himself into Design P, the 'additions' are recorded via the owner's current account as an amount payable to Mr P. Mr P is caught as soon as the auditor questions the rationale and commercial substance of having 15 graphic design computers (five sets are on the original records plus the ten additions) for only five designers on Design P's payroll. The additions make no commercial sense and can only be explained as assets purely for non-business purposes. Bearing no impact on revenues, assets are overstated, and possibly paired with an overstatement of amount due to shareholders (liability).

INFLATING UNIT VALUE OF TANGIBLE FIXED ASSETS

We now consider the unit value of fixed assets. An asset is impaired when its carrying amount exceeds its recoverable amount.[5] A fixed asset should not be carried in the B/S at more than its recoverable amount and is recognized at its carrying amount in the B/S after deducting any accumulated depreciation (amortization) and accumulated impairment losses thereon. Recoverable amount is the higher of an asset's net selling price and the amount recoverable from its future use. An organization should assess at each financial year-end whether there is any indication that an asset may be impaired.

In accordance with the Companies Act 1985 in the UK, the treatment of impairment (or diminution in value) is as follows:

- assets held at cost:
  - temporary diminutions are not recognized;
  - permanent diminutions are recognized and charged to the P&L.

- assets held at valuation:
  - temporary diminutions are recognized and charged (debited) to reserves;
  - permanent diminutions are recognized and charged (debited) to the asset's previous surplus in reserves and then to the P&L for the financial year.

Where an increase in value relates to the reversal of a permanent diminution in value previously charged to the P&L, the increase will be credited to the P&L for the current financial year.

In Hong Kong, the Companies Ordinance requires provisions to be made to assets as and when any amount is written off or retained by way of providing for depreciation, renewals or diminution in value of assets. This is similar to the definition of impairment loss which is the amount by which the carrying amount of an asset exceeds its recoverable amount as defined in SSAP 31 of the HKICPA and FRS 11 of the ASB. A review for impairment of a fixed asset or goodwill should be carried out if events or changes in circumstances indicate that the carrying amount of the fixed asset or goodwill may not be recoverable.

However, the Companies Act 1985 does not provide guidance on how the recoverable amount should be measured and when impairment losses should be recognized. As a result, some impairment may not be recognized on a timely basis. Tangible fixed assets and goodwill are recorded in the financial statements at no more than their recoverable amount. Any resulting impairment loss is measured and recognized on a consistent basis.[6]

Impairment occurs due to one of two things:[7]

- something happening to the tangible fixed asset itself, such as:
  - a significant downturn in the property market; or

- something occurring in the environment within which the asset operates, such as:
  - fire or water damage to an asset;
  - a significant drop in the utilization of an organization's factory; or
  - a change of purpose of any organization's manufacturing plant from the manufacturing of key products to processing by-products of lower profit margin.

The impairment review consists of a comparison of the carrying amount of the tangible fixed asset with its recoverable amount (the higher of net realizable value, if known, and value in use).[8] To the extent that the carrying amount exceeds the recoverable amount, the tangible fixed asset is impaired and should be written down. The impairment loss should be recognized in the P&L unless it arises on previous revalued fixed assets.

Compliance with SSAP 31 of the HKICPA and FRS 11 of the ASB (subject to certain exceptions[9]) ensures compliance in all material respects with International Accounting Standard IAS 36 *Impairment of Assets.*

Let us consider a relevant case.

CASE 5.2

OBSOLETE RAILWAY TRACK

P Ltd operates a power station and has a private railway designed to transport raw materials from the port to the power station. The private railway does not have a resale value, that is, it has a zero scrap value.

According to a consultant's report, the transportation costs for delivery by truck from a new port closer to the power station is lower than the transportation costs using the railway. The consultant's report indicates a potential impairment of the railway and puts forward a write-down of the railway to zero as the private railway does not generate cash inflows from continuing use.

However, the report recommends keeping the railway for contingencies, which requires a consideration of the cash inflows from the other assets of the power station. Used together with other assets of the power station (as contingencies), the value of the private railway to P Ltd is likely to be higher than its zero scrap value. It is not possible to determine the recoverable amount of the railway separately. P Ltd should estimate the recoverable amount of the cash-generating unit to which the private railway belongs, which is the power station as a whole.

DELAYING DEPRECIATION OR AMORTIZATION OF TANGIBLE FIXED ASSETS

Depreciation is the systematic allocating of the depreciable amount of an asset over its estimated useful life.[10] Accumulated depreciation is a deduction from the cost or revalued amount of the fixed assets. Thus, the lower the accumulated depreciation is, the higher the carrying value would be. In other words, assets can be overstated by having lower expenses of depreciation or amortization. Suppressing depreciation is discussed in Chapter 4 as an example of understatement of expenditure.

INVENTORIES

Inventories refer to assets which are:[11]

- held for sale in the ordinary course of business;

- in the process of production for such sale; or

- in the form of materials or supplies to be consumed in the production process or in the rendering of services.

The term 'inventories' is equivalent to 'stocks' used in SSAP 9 of the ASB as goods purchased for resale, consumable stores, materials purchased for incorporation into products for sale, products and services in intermediate stages of completion, and finished goods.

The three components of the cost of inventories are costs of purchase, costs of conversion and other costs incurred in bringing the inventories to their present location and condition.[12]

Costs of purchase comprise:

- purchase price (excluding trade discounts, rebates and subsidies);
- import duties and other irrecoverable taxes;
- inwards transportation and handling costs, and
- any other directly attributable costs.

Costs of conversion relate to the production process and include direct labour and direct materials. They also include a systematic allocation of fixed and variable production overheads that are incurred in converting raw materials into finished goods. Other costs may include non-production overheads or the costs of designing products for specific customers in the cost of inventories.

Compliance with SSAP 22 of the HKICPA or SSAP 9 of the ASB ensures compliance with IAS 2 *Inventories* in all material respects. The only substantial difference is that IAS 2 allows the LIFO (last-in-first-out) method to be adopted for the valuation of inventory, so long as certain additional disclosures are provided. Neither SSAP 22 of the HKICPA nor SSAP 9 of the ASB strictly prohibits the use of LIFO, but they both make clear that it is rarely going to be an appropriate method to use.

In essence, inventories represent raw materials, work-in-progress and finished goods and are recorded in the B/S as an asset (current asset). When the inventory is sold, its cost is transferred to the P&L and reported as cost of sales (or cost of goods sold). An overstatement of inventory has the equivalent effect of understating cost of sales which means overstated profitability.

As inventory increases, so do current assets and the apparent liquidity and solvency. By reducing cost of sales, perpetrators' gross profit margin and net profit are overstated.

Similar to tangible fixed assets, the inventories in the B/S are reported by two components – quantities and unit value, thus:

$$\text{Total value} = \text{Quantities} \times \text{Unit value}$$

Therefore, in overstating the inventories, perpetrators may manipulate either of these two components. There are at least three ways to do so:

- overstating physical count of inventories

- inflating unit value of inventories

- delaying write-off of inventories.

Let us consider each of them in turn.

OVERSTATING PHYSICAL COUNT OF INVENTORIES

As with tangible fixed assets, one way of overstating inventories is to manipulate the physical count and to record fictitious quantities of inventories. This false creation of assets affects the reported value of inventories in an organization's B/S. If an organization's inventories are located in many different sites, this kind of accounting irregularity can easily be overlooked. In addition, perpetrators may try shifting inventories between different locations at or around the financial year-end. It creates confusion as to which location the inventories in transit should have been recorded and causes duplication in recording the inventories. The problem is made more difficult to discover when inventories at different locations are audited by different persons.

Overstating the physical count may involve fabrication of inventory count sheets, goods receipt notes, dispatch notes and related reports. Some perpetrators may deliberately make errors in adding up individual items in the lengthy inventory reports so as to inflate the overall inventory quantities.

Another irregular way to overstate the physical quantity of inventories is to neglect customers' returns and to regard scrap, defective or returned items as in good condition. As introduced in Chapter 3, there are 'bill and hold' sales of which inventories are sold but kept in an organization's warehouse for future delivery to customers. It is irregular to include those items in the physical inventory count.

Also, goods owned by third parties but held by the organization on consignment (or for storage) might still be included in the physical inventory count. By adjusting inventory dispatches and receipts a few days before and after the financial year-end date, the cut-offs of inventories, sales and purchases are manipulated to the desired figures. Understated sales increase inventories (also overstating revenues and assets), while overstated purchases also increase inventories.

Some cases in this area involve bribery and conspiracy. For example, an accomplice may claim to hold inventory for the organization in question. Of course, it is possible to put up fake inventories on the shelves pretending to be genuine items. It may be difficult for the auditor to find out. Let us consider a relevant case.

CASE 5.3

EMPTY BOXES OF INVENTORY

P Ltd is a takeover target of a multinational group. As a defensive strategy, the directors of P Ltd want to boost the value of P Ltd in order to justify to the existing shareholders that the offer price is far too low. P Ltd's sales in 2004 and 2005 are $6 400 000 and $6 350 000 respectively, and the gross profit increases from $1 050 000 to $1 200 000.

$750 000 worth of inventories are recorded in the B/S at the end of 2005, representing a 50 per cent increase from 2004. Extracts from P Ltd's financial statements are shown in Table 5.1.

Table 5.1   Overstated inventory

P Ltd: Extracts from financial statements

	Adjusted amounts (regular) 2005 $000	Initial amounts (irregular) 2005 $000	Actual amounts 2004 $000
Sales	6 400	6 400	6 350
Cost of sales	5 350	5 200	5 300
Gross profit	1 050	1 200	1 050
Inventories in B/S	600	750	500
Gross profit margin	16.4%	18.8%	16.5%
Inventory turnover days	41 days	53 days	34 days

P Ltd makes up pallets of inventories with hollow centres, places bricks in sealed boxes instead of high value products, and shifts inventories overnight between locations being inspected by auditors on different days, so as to double-count the inventories. P Ltd also inserts fraudulent count sheets during the inventory verification check or changes the quantities on the count sheets.

The auditors are suspicious about the significant increase of the inventory turnover days from 34 days to 53 days. However, P Ltd is caught because the auditors make copies of the count sheets that are used during the inventory verification check. The discrepancies are revealed through a straightforward comparison between the two piles of count sheets which are supposedly identical. The impact of the accounting irregularity is that the profits and inventories in 2005 are both overstated by $150 000, at $1 200 000 and $750 000 respectively.

INFLATING UNIT VALUE OF INVENTORIES

As well as overstating the physical count, a higher unit value can also inflate the inventories.

In Chapter 4, we discussed the possibility of understating expenditure by overstating the inventory valuation. During the time of a general increase in pricing levels, changing the inventory valuation method from average cost (or LIFO, applicable in limited cases only) to FIFO would suppress the cost of sales. This would have a corresponding (but opposite) impact on inventory carrying value – overstating the inventory unit value.

In service organizations, unbilled services that are classified as work-in-progress may not necessarily be fully recoverable and therefore should have a reduced carrying value.

A long-term contract is defined as a contract entered into for the construction of a single substantial asset where the time taken to complete the contract is such that the contract activity falls into different financial years.[13] A similar term is used to define construction contracts in SSAP 23 *Construction Contract* (issued by the HKICPA in May 1998, revised January 2001, effective for accounting periods starting on or after 1 January 1998). Compliance with SSAP 9 of the ASB and SSAP 31 of the HKICPA ensures compliance with International Accounting Standard IAS 11 *Construction Contracts*.

In a long-term contract, sales and profit are recognized as the contract progresses.[14] Sales are determined in a manner appropriate to the stage of completion of the contract, the business and the industry. Profit is recognized as part of the total profit estimated to arise over the duration of the contract that fairly reflects the profit attributable to that part of the work performed at the financial year-end date.

An accounting irregularity of this kind may be to mis-state the stage of completion of long-term contracts to recognize revenues earlier than is acceptable under GAAP. This causes timing difference of overstating revenues and assets in the early periods, even though the total amount of revenues over the life of each long-term contract remains the same. Similarly, completed work-in-progress is recognized as completed and invoiced before delivery to customers. This means an overstatement in inventories.

Let us consider a relevant case.

CASE 5.4

CREATIVITY IN INVENTORY VALUATION

P Ltd starts its business in 2004. At the end of 2004, P Ltd's B/S is summarized in Table 5.2.

Table 5.2   Inventory creativity – B/S

P Ltd: Balance sheet as at 31 December 2004

	2004 $
Fixed assets	30 000
Current assets:	
Inventories	8 000
Debtors	3 000
Cash at banks	4 000
	45 000
Creditors: amount falling due within a year	5 500
Creditors: amount falling due after more than one year	6 500
Ordinary shares	33 000
Profit & loss account	0
	45 000

The average cost inventory valuation method is deemed to be most appropriate for P Ltd's nature of business and has been adopted for many years. However, P Ltd is under pressure to increase its net worth and profitability and changes the inventory valuation method to FIFO during 2005.

The opening and closing inventory quantities, purchases and sales of units during 2005 are shown in Table 5.3.

There are 350 units sold in 2005 with 250 units of closing inventories on 31 December 2005. P Ltd tries an aggressive way of valuing these units of inventories in order to irregularly maximize its profits. A comparison of the three alternative inventory valuation methods is set out in Table 5.4.

Table 5.3 Inventory creativity – movements

P Ltd: Movements of inventories in 2005

		Quantities	Unit cost $	Total $
Opening inventory	1-Jan-05	200	3.50	7 000
Purchase	3-Feb-05	100	4.50	4 500
Purchase	15-Mar-05	100	5.50	5 500
Purchase	19-May-05	100	6.00	6 000
Purchase	21-Jul-05	100	7.00	7 000
Units available for sale		600		30 000
Units sold during 2005		(350)		
Closing inventory on 31-Dec-05		250		

Table 5.4 Inventory creativity – P&L

P Ltd: Extracts from profit and loss account under three alternative inventory valuation methods

	Average cost method $	FIFO $	LIFO $
Sales (350 units sold at $80 each)	28 000	28 000	28 000
Cost of sales:			
Opening inventory	8 000	8 000	8 000
Purchase	22 000	22 000	22 000
Closing inventory	(12 500)	(14 750)	(10 250)
Cost of sales total	17 500	15 250	19 750
Gross profit	10 500	12 750	8 250

P Ltd's gross profit is $10 500 (under the average cost inventory valuation method). By changing it to FIFO, P Ltd's gross profit increases by $2250 to $12 750. P Ltd's B/S as prepared under each of the three alternative inventory valuation methods is set out in Table 5.5.

Table 5.5   Inventory creativity – valuation methods

P Ltd: Extracts from balance sheet under three alternative inventory valuation methods

	2005 *Average cost method* $	2005 *FIFO* $	2005 $	2004 *LIFO* $
Fixed assets	30 000	30 000	30 000	30 000
Current assets:				
Inventories	12 500	14 750	10 250	8 000
Debtors	3 000	3 000	3 000	3 000
Cash at banks	10 000	10 000	10 000	4 000
	55 500	57 750	53 250	45 000
Creditors:				
Amount falling due within a year	5 500	5 500	5 500	5 500
Creditors:				
Amount falling due after more than one year	6 500	6 500	6 500	6 500
Ordinary shares	33 000	33 000	33 000	33 000
Profit & loss account	10 500	12 750	8 250	0
	55 500	57 750	53 250	45 000

It is important to note that this case is a grey area as both average cost and FIFO are acceptable under the GAAP in Hong Kong and the UK. It is irregular in the sense that P Ltd has an intention to massage the financial statements to the preferred figures (it is often known as 'creative accounting' – see Chapter 2).

DELAYING WRITE-OFF OF INVENTORIES

Inventories should be measured at the lower of cost and net realizable value (NRV).[15] At each financial year-end, the carrying value of inventories which is presumably at cost must be compared to NRV. Cost includes those costs incurred in the normal course of business in bringing a product or service to its present location and condition.[16] NRV is the actual or estimated selling price less further costs to be incurred in marketing, selling and distribution.[17]

The cost of inventories may not be recoverable if:[18]

● those inventories are damaged;

- they become wholly or partially obsolete;

- their selling prices decline; or

- the estimated costs of completion, or the estimated costs to be incurred to conclude the sales, increase.

Writing inventories down below cost to NRV is consistent with the view that assets should not be carried in excess of amounts expected to be realized from their sale or use.

By delaying the write-off of inventories that are damaged, obsolete or slow-moving, perpetrators may overvalue inventory. Failing to write off inventory results in overstated assets and the mismatching of cost of sales with revenues, and it is of course in violation of GAAP.

Inventories are usually written down to NRV on an item-by-item basis rather than on the basis of the entire classification of inventories such as finished goods. If this is impracticable, groups of similar items may be considered together. This may be the case when items of inventory:[19]

- relate to the same product line that have similar purposes or end users;

- are produced and marketed in the same geographical area; and

- cannot be practicably evaluated separately from other items in that product line.

Raw materials held for use in the production of inventories are written down to NRV (with reference to the replacement costs)[20] if the finished goods in which the raw materials are incorporated are expected to be sold at a loss. Under the matching concept, costs must be allocated between the cost of sales (matched against current revenues) and closing inventories (matched against future revenues).[21]

Compliance with SSAP 22 of the HKICPA and SSAP 9 of the ASB ensures compliance with International Accounting Standard IAS 2 *Inventories*.

TRADE DEBTORS

Trade debtors or account receivables are subject to manipulation similar to sales and inventories, and in many cases, differences amongst accounting irregularities of these kinds are often not clear. There are at least two irregular ways of overstating trade debtors:

- fictitious receivables;

- failure to write off account receivables as bad debts (failure to establish an adequate provision for bad or doubtful debts).

FICTITIOUS RECEIVABLES

Fictitious receivables are usually associated with fictitious revenues, which are discussed in Chapter 3. Fictitious receivables occur most often in organizations in financial difficulties, as well as those where the perpetrators receive a sales-based commission. The typical entry under fictitious receivables are to debit (increase) account receivables and to credit (increase) sales. These schemes are more common at or around the financial year-end because account receivables are expected to remain outstanding for a reasonable period of time (the duration of credit term). Similarly, loan documentations are fabricated, and loans are made to fictitious parties. That gives an overstatement of account receivables and an understatement of cash at bank.

Let us consider a relevant case.

CASE 5.5

FICTITIOUS RECEIVABLES FROM DUMMY CUSTOMERS

Mr P is the sales director of a carpet manufacturer and fitter and receives regular bonuses linked with the sales revenue. Mr P abuses his power by creating several dummy customers' accounts. Shortly before the financial year-end, Mr P creates a series of fictitious sales with these dummy customers. Mr P tries to conceal fictitious account receivables by providing false confirmations of balances to auditors.

The audit confirmations are sent and returned duly signed because mailboxes under Mr P's control, Mr P's own home address or the business address of Mr P's accomplice are used as the mailing address of the dummy customers.

Ultimately, Mr P is caught when such schemes are detected by using business credit reports, public records and telephone books to identify significant customers with no physical existence or no apparent business need for the carpets sold to them.

FAILURE TO WRITE OFF

Trade debtors are stated at the net amount expected to be received on collection, which calls for an estimate of irrecoverable amounts (provision for doubtful debts).

When there are indications of some or all of a particular trade debtor account becoming irrecoverable, the irrecoverable portion should be charged against the provision for doubtful debts in the P&L. Subsequently, if the provision for doubtful debts is not inadequate to cater for actual irrecoverable accounts, an additional provision or bad debt write-off will be required to accommodate the additional irrecoverable amounts. If bad debts are not written off, or doubtful debts are not provided for, assets are irregularly overstated whereas expenses are irregularly understated.

There are at least two bases in calculating the provision for doubtful debts:

- as a consistent proportion of total debtors;

- as a progressive proportion according to the ageing of respective debtors.

No matter how good an organization's credit policy is, there are uncontrollable factors and bad debts may emerge. The longer the debt has been outstanding the less chance there is of its being recovered and thus the greater the chance of its requiring a provision. Some organizations may therefore provide against all debts over a certain age and then make provisions against the younger debts on a reducing scale.

Some perpetrators may use the provision for doubtful debts as a profit-smoothing device. A general provision is gradually built up while profits are high. When the business is not so good, the perpetrator is able to use the provision to absorb some of the impact by stopping any further additional provisions and releasing (or writing back) a part of the provision on the ground that the provision is no longer necessary.

CONCLUSION

The figures of assets (less liabilities) on an organization's B/S are sometimes perceived as an important indication in business valuation and an approximation of the net worth of the organization. Accordingly, the more assets an organization records, the higher its business appears to be worth.

Learning from experience, organizations should stay alert for certain warning signs that may indicate possible accounting irregularities in the overstatement of assets. To end this chapter, typical warning signs are set out for reference:

- abnormally high level of assets in comparison with the organization's historical average and/or the industry benchmark;

- significant transactions with related parties or other entities not in the ordinary course of business or where those entities are unaudited or audited by a different auditor;

- unusual or highly complex transactions whose substance and ownership is not known, especially those close to financial year-end;

- unusual increase in assets recorded only in certain business units which are not shared by other parts of the same organization;

- gaps in the sequence of asset serial numbers, vendors' invoices and title documents;

- missing originals of important documents, such as receipts, contracts and title deeds;

- the lack of third-party or consignment inventories which contradicts the organization's past operation and/or the industry norm; and

- neglect or ignorance of the importance of reviewing the condition of assets (the cost of inventories may be lower than their resale value).

Notes

1, 2 – SSAP 29 *Intangible Assets* (issued by the HKICPA in January 2001, effective for accounting periods starting on or after 1 January 2001). The HKICPA is the successor to the Hong Kong Society of Accountants (HKSA)

3, 4, 9 – SSAP 17 *Property, Plant & Equipment* (issued by the HKICPA in July 1995, revised April 2001, effective for accounting periods starting on or after 1 January 2001)

4 – FRS 15 *Tangible Fixed Assets* (issued by the ASB in February 1999, effective for accounting periods starting on or after 23 March 2000). The ASB is the successor to the Accounting Standards Committee (ASC)

5 – SSAP 31 *Impairment of Assets* (issued by the HKICPA in January 2001, effective for accounting periods starting on or after 1 January 2001)

6, 7, 8 – FRS 11 *Impairment of Fixed Assets and Goodwill* (issued by the ASB in July 1998, effective for accounting periods ending on or after 23 December 1998)

9 – Appendix III of FRS 11 *Impairment of Fixed Assets and Goodwill* (issued by the ASB in July 1998, effective for accounting periods ending on or after 23 December 1998)

10 – FRS 15 *Tangible Fixed Assets* (issued by the ASB in February 1999, effective for accounting periods starting on or after 23 March 2000)

11, 13, 15, 16, 18, 19, 20 – SSAP 22 *Inventory* (issued by the HKICPA in May 1998, revised January 2001, effective for accounting periods starting on or after 1 January 1998)

12, 13, 14, 15, 16, 17, 21 – SSAP 9 *Stocks and Long-term Contracts* (issued by the ASB in May 1975, revised August 1980 and September 1988, effective for accounting periods starting on or after 1 July 1988)

14 – SSAP 31 *Impairment of Assets* (issued by the HKICPA in January 2001, effective for accounting periods starting on or after 1 January 2001)

CHAPTER 6

Owing Less

UNDERSTATEMENT OF LIABILITIES

'Owing less' is what drives some perpetrators. By understating the liabilities of an organization, perpetrators try to create a situation where the organization appears to owe less than it actually does. Defining the correct figure of an organization's liabilities should be done with reference to the appropriate generally accepted accounting principles (GAAP). Any departure from these are deemed to be irregular (accounting irregularities).

In gauging the amount of an organization's net assets, total liabilities are deducted from total assets. Accounting irregularities of owing less sometimes occur together with overstatement of assets as set out in Chapter 5. Keeping other variables intact, the understatement of an organization's liabilities portrays an illusion of having more net resources than the organization in question actually has. In essence, the degree of an organization's future sacrifices (in terms of future settlement of its present obligation) is suppressed.

RELEVANT GAAP IN HONG KONG AND THE UK

In Hong Kong, there are two main reference points for the accounting treatment of liabilities. The first one is the *Framework for the Preparation and Presentation of Financial Statements* (Framework), issued by the HKICPA in June 1997 (revised May 2003). Also, SSAP 28 *Provisions, Contingent Liabilities and Contingent Assets* was issued by the HKICPA in January 2001, effective for accounting periods starting on or after 1 January 2001.

Liabilities are defined as a present obligation (not a future commitment) which refers to a duty or responsibility to act or perform in a certain way arising from a binding contract or statutory requirement.[1] Liabilities arise from past transactions or other past events, such as buying goods and services which creates an obligation to pay, giving rise to account payables or trade creditors. Trade creditors are liabilities to pay for goods or services that have been delivered and invoiced. Having a bank overdraft or utilizing a bank credit facility also creates an obligation to repay the loan. Accruals are liabilities to pay for goods or services that have been delivered but have not been invoiced by the vendors. Some liabilities, known as provisions, can only be measured by estimation.

Accruals and provisions are similar in nature. In the UK, FRS 12 *Provisions, Contingent Liabilities and Contingent Assets*, issued by the ASB in December 1999, effective for accounting periods ending on or after 23 March 1999, states that a liability is an organization's obligation to transfer economic benefits as a result of past transactions or events. A provision is a liability of uncertain timing or amount.

A provision differs from other liabilities in the sense that the degree of uncertainty about the timing or amount of the future expenditure is generally higher than accruals.[2] For example, amounts due to employees relating to accrued leave pay are based on estimation and are generally regarded as accruals. Although it is sometimes necessary to estimate the amount or timing of accruals, the uncertainty is generally much less than the uncertainty of provisions. Provisions are separately disclosed in a balance sheet under the headings of liabilities.

Accounting for liabilities involves various aspects in accounting and GAAP, such as:

- Provisions and contingent liabilities and the appropriate accounting treatments are primarily determined on the basis of:
  - SSAP 28 *Provisions, Contingent Liabilities and Contingent Assets* (issued by the HKICPA in January 2001, effective for accounting periods starting on or after 1 January 2001)
  - FRS 12 *Provisions, Contingent Liabilities and Contingent Assets* (issued by the ASB in December 1999, effective for accounting periods ending on or after 23 March 1999).

- Employees' benefits and the appropriate accounting treatments are primarily determined on the basis of:
  - SSAP 34 *Employee Benefits* (issued by the HKICPA in May 2003, effective for accounting periods starting on or after 1 January 2002)
  - FRS 17 *Retirement Benefits* (issued by the ASB in November 2000, effective for accounting periods ending on or after 22 June 2005).

- Off-balance-sheet financing and the appropriate accounting treatments are primarily determined on the basis of:
  - SSAP 14 *Leases* (issued by the HKICPA in October 1987, revised February 2000, effective for accounting periods starting on or after 1 July 2000)
  - SSAP 21 *Accounting for Leases and Hire Purchase Contracts* (issued by the ASB in August 1984, amended February 1997, effective for accounting periods starting on or after 1 July 1984)
  - FRS 5 *Substance of Transactions* (issued by the ASB in April 1994, amended December 1994 and September 1998, effective for accounting periods ending on or after 22 September 1994).

A detailed examination of the above standards would go beyond the scope of this book, and readers are encouraged to refer to the original texts for a more advanced study of these subjects. It is important to remember the basics of accounting irregularities and the double-entry book-keeping regime as introduced in Chapter 2.

If expenses of the current financial year in the P&L which are not settled are understated, so too will be the corresponding liabilities in the B/S. Chapters 3 and 4 include some discussions of accounting irregularities in overstating revenue and understating expenditure, which are closely related to the understatement of liabilities.

Let us consider the appropriate GAAP and review some aggressive attempts in suppressing the reported liabilities in organizations' financial statements. The sequence of our discussion in this chapter follows four categories of liabilities:

- trade creditors

- accruals and provisions

- contingent liabilities

- off-balance-sheet financing.

TRADE CREDITORS

Trade creditors represent liabilities to pay for items which have been received and invoiced. Similar to off-book expenditure (see Chapter 4), one way of concealing liabilities is simply not to record them.

Trade creditors result from purchases of goods or services for which payments have not been made. Rather than posting the purchases, suppliers' invoices might be destroyed or deliberately withheld (even though the suppliers are likely to send copy invoices later). Thus, profits in the P&L are overstated whereas trade creditors in the B/S are understated, by the same amount. In addition, the cut-off procedures at or around the financial year-end may be manipulated in a similar way as 'revocable sales' which were introduced in Chapter 3.

As both the trade creditors and purchases are understated, the costs of sales are also suppressed, assuring that the opening balance of inventories is accurate. Costs of sales equate to the inventories at the start of a financial year plus purchases and direct manufacturing costs minus the inventories at the end of that financial year. Therefore, subtracting accurate closing inventories from the understated purchases gives a higher profit figure in the P&L. When those concealed inventory purchases are discovered at a later stage, a charge would then be made to the P&L together with a liability recorded in the B/S.

To check whether all the trade creditors are stated in the financial statements, the auditors often review the list of major suppliers. In some cases, an organization relies heavily on one major supplier. The reason may simply be that an established relationship exists between an organization and a particular supplier. However, the relationship may become questionable when there are many other suppliers with comparable products that could be substituted. Another possible explanation is that, if one supplier is so valuable to an organization, perhaps that supplier is a related party.

ACCRUALS AND PROVISIONS

Accruals are also liabilities to pay for goods or services that have been delivered, but unlike trade creditors, the liabilities have not yet been invoiced by the vendor. As a result, the unpaid amount is accrued as a liability on the B/S. Examples are numerous, such as salaries, utility bills, audit fees and purchases of inventories. Some expenses, on the other hand, rarely require accruals, such as rent and insurance premiums (which are normally payable in advance).

When there is an understatement of accruals in one period, the level of expenses in future periods is bound to be higher because, as soon as these additional expenses are discovered, a payment is required to settle an obligation for which no liability has been accrued.

SSAP 28 of the HKICPA defines a liability in the same way as the Framework, and the settlement of a liability is expected to result in an outflow of economic benefits; provisions are a subset of liabilities. A liability is an organization's obligation to transfer economic benefits as a result of past transactions or events.[3] A provision is a liability of uncertain timing or amount.[4] Provisions are separately disclosed in a B/S under the heading of liabilities. Accruals and provisions are similar in nature. While uncertainty is inevitably present in certain cases of accruals, the uncertainty is generally much less than for provisions.

Chapter 4 dealt with the understatement of expenditure which often coincides with an understatement of liabilities. Let us consider a relevant case about provisions and how perpetrators might use them to understate an organization's liabilities.

CASE 6.1

MISSING LIABILITIES

P Group is a conglomerate comprising three main lines of business and tries to minimize the recording of liabilities as much as possible, even if it means committing accounting irregularities. Three accounting irregularities are found as follows:

- Manufacture of electronic device – P Group manufactures an electronic device and sells to customers together with warranties. Under the terms of the sale contract, P Group undertakes to make good, by repair or replacement, any manufacturing defects that become apparent within three years from the date of sale.

- Retail store – the retail store business of P Group has a policy of refunding any return by dissatisfied customers within seven days, even though there is no legal obligation to do so. Its policy of making refunds is generally known.

- Chemical production – P Group's chemical production process causes contamination. It is P Group's policy not to clean up any contamination unless required to do so by law. One third-world country in which it operates has no legislation requiring cleaning up, and P Group has been contaminating land in that country for several years. In January 2005 (between P Group's current financial year-end in 2004 and the approval of its financial statements), a law is passed requiring existing owners to clean up their land which has already been contaminated.

P Group is guilty of not accruing for liabilities in respect of the three above matters. These are accounting irregularities because:

- Manufacture of electronic device – P Group's electronic device is sold with a warranty: an event which gives rise to a legal obligation. P Group is likely to face some claims under the warranties. There may well be an outflow of resources embodying economic benefits; a provision should be recognized for the best estimate of the costs of making good under the warranty products sold before the financial year-end.

- Retail store – similarly, P Group sells the product with a refunding policy: an event which gives rise to a constructive obligation because the conduct of the store has created a valid expectation on the part of its customers that the store would refund any return within seven days. Since it is probable that a proportion of goods are returned for refund, a provision for sales return should be recognized for the best estimate of the amount of refunds. As introduced in Chapter 3 (Case 3.11), by publicly announcing its refund policy, P Group creates a valid expectation on the part of customers that its policy of refunds would be honoured. There is a constructive obligation on the organization to meet the refund costs and a provision for the expected returns should be recognized.[5] The facts in Case 3.11 should be contrasted with the situation for a retailer as in this case in which a refund policy is offered to its customers. Since

> P Group as a retailer is usually in a position to predict the probability of goods returns based on previous experience and other relevant factors, revenue should be recognized at the point of sale.
>
> • Chemical substance production – P Group's contamination of the land is the obligating event. In January 2005, between the relevant financial year-end and the approval of the financial statements, it is clear that the new legislation requires cleaning up the land, and a provision should be recognized for the best estimate of the costs of this.

Before SSAP 28 of the HKICPA and FRS 12 of the ASB, there were no formal GAAP dealing with provisions. Some organizations wanting to show their results in the most favourable light made large one-off provisions in years when the profits were good and healthy. These provisions were then available to shield expenditure in future years when perhaps the underlying profits were not as good. In other words, provisions were used as a profit-smoothing device, and this kind of aggressive practice has now been ruled out by SSAP 28 of the HKICPA and FRS 12 of the ASB.

In the past, it was quite popular to accrue or provide for expenditure on a major repair overhaul gradually over the years between overhauls. This is no longer permitted since it is merely an intention (rather than an obligation) to carry out repairs.[6]

In addition, some organizations operated their own self-insurance policies and created a provision on the basis of the expected cost of making good after an interruption (such as a fire or flood) instead of paying premiums to an external insurer. This provision is no longer permitted since the organization has no obligation until an interruption occurs.[7]

Compliance with SSAP 28 of the HKICPA and FRS 12 of the ASB ensure compliance with IAS 37 *Provisions, Contingent Liabilities and Contingent Assets* in all material aspects. There are no significant differences amongst the three standards.

Another major area in accruals and provisions involves employees' benefits. Employees' benefits are all forms of consideration given by an organization in exchange of employees' services.[8] Employees' benefits can be categorized into four types:[9]

- short-term employee benefits
- long-term employee benefits
- terminal benefits
- equity compensation benefits.

In the UK, FRS 17 of the ASB deals with all retirement benefits that an employer is committed to providing, whether the commitment is statutory, contractual or implicit in the employer's actions. The underlying principles in accruing and providing for employees' benefits remain the same as in other areas.

Compliance with SSAP 34 of the HKICPA and FRS 17 of the ASB ensure compliance with IAS 19 *Employee Benefits* in all material aspects. There are no significant differences amongst the three standards.

CONTINGENT LIABILITIES

A contingent liability refers to:[10]

- a possible obligation that arises from past events and whose existence will be confirmed only by the occurrence or non-occurrence of one or more uncertain future events not wholly within the organization's control; or

- a present obligation that arises from past events but is not recognized because:

    - it is not probable that an outflow of economic benefits will be required to settle the obligation; or

    - the amount of the obligation cannot be measured with sufficient reliability.

As a rule of thumb, 'probable' means more than 50 per cent likelihood. If an obligation is probable, it requires a provision, rather than being treated as a contingent liability. Contingent liabilities are not recognized, but they should be disclosed in the notes to the financial statements.

Examples of contingent liabilities include a claim arising from a commercial dispute and possible award by the courts. One way is to simply hide or disguise the claims or lawsuits in the hope that no one ever finds out. However, the customers (complainants) and claimants do not easily give up and will try every possible way to get their cases heard. Thus, the auditor may easily find out. The cost of cleaning up environmental damage caused by an organization is another example, where before completion the total cost of a clean-up cannot be known with certainty. Reading the Notes and understanding an organization's business can help to determine if there are any undisclosed contingent liabilities.

Due to the nature and available evidence of contingent liabilities, perpetrators may find it easier to commit accounting irregularities involving contingent liabilities. Apart from litigative losses, there are other types of contingent liabilities including:

- Loan covenants – these are agreements that a borrower has promised to keep as long as the financing is in place. The agreements can contain various types of covenants including certain financial ratio limits and restrictions on other major financing arrangements, and any violation of these will usually trigger the immediate repayment of the loan. Contingent liabilities deriving from loan covenants are potential obligations that the organization in question would face only if certain triggering events occur in the future.

- Guarantees of subsidiary credit lines – where a bank lends to a subsidiary within a group, it normally requires a guarantee from the holding entity. Without such a guarantee, if the subsidiary gets into difficulties, the holding entity will only be liable to the extent that there are amounts paid in respect of its shareholding in the subsidiary, leaving the bank with the loss. Such a guarantee is a contingent liability to the holding entity.

- Performance bonds – in the construction industry, a property developer is often required to give a bond from its bank to ensure that the standard of certain matters (such as roads and drains on an estate complex being constructed) is acceptable to the local community and authority. Since the bank will usually require the property developer to provide a counter guarantee, the property developer therefore has a contingent liability to its bank if the bond is ever called.

OFF-BALANCE-SHEET FINANCING

Off-balance-sheet financing refers to a way of raising funds without reflecting those borrowings in an organization's B/S. Leasing is a classic example of off-balance-sheet financing. In the 1970–80s, leasing was widely used as an off-balance-sheet financing device.

Rather than buying an asset, an organization may choose to lease it instead. Previously, by leasing (rather than buying) the asset, an organization would have been able to ignore the recording of the asset and lease liability in its B/S. Thus, potentially large liabilities were off the B/S. These omissions may mislead readers of the organizations' financial statements which indicate understated levels of assets and liabilities.

Off-balance-sheet financing was attractive for a number of reasons. Leverage (gearing) ratio (the proportion of net borrowings to shareholders' funds) tends to be low for organizations in Hong Kong and the UK compared with those in the US and some other countries. Off-balance-sheet financing is used to keep the leverage low within the terms of loan covenants imposed by lenders and in meeting financial market expectations. Off-balance-sheet financing may also be a way to reduce the leverage to a comfortable level before a rights issue, so that the organization's share price is at a more favourable rate and more additional capital can be raised.

For an organization operating in the form of a group of companies, it may want to exclude certain subsidiaries from consolidation because they carry completely different types of business and have different characteristics. As an off-balance-sheet financing device, those subsidiaries' liabilities are therefore not reflected in the group's consolidated B/S (see the subsequent section on quasi-subsidiaries).

The financial market is well aware of the dangers of a high level of debts. When the leverage ratio of an organization becomes excessively high, the financial market may become alarmed and the organization's share price may dip as a result. The management might be tempted to enter into off-balance-sheet financing devices in bringing down the leverage ratio.

Let us consider a relevant case.

CASE 6.2

IRREGULAR BANKING ARRANGEMENT

A merchant bank (Bank P) identifies an organization which has a high level of leverage that is close to the limit imposed by its articles of association or shareholders' agreement. Bank P approaches the organization's management and suggests an off-balance-sheet financing scheme which allows the organization to increase its borrowings without breaching the articles of association. The organization's management accepts the scheme because this would save the embarrassment of having to go to the shareholders to ask for a change in the articles of association.

This may be very convenient for the management but it undermines the reason for those articles. The limits are to ensure that management, which runs the organization on behalf of shareholders, does not commit to unrealistic and impractical levels of debts. By having such an off-balance-sheet financing scheme in place, the control that shareholders have over the organization's management has disappeared.

By and large, off-balance-sheet financing offers practical solutions to commercial problems. Some argue that shareholders and other readers of financial statements are really not deceived since the missing liabilities are matched by the missing assets. There is no doubt that off-balance-sheet financing, in whatever form, distorts the true state of a business and might mislead readers of financial statements.

The main attraction of off-balance-sheet financing is that it allows an organization to secure borrowings without showing the liabilities. If the substance of a transaction is to secure borrowings, then those borrowings should be shown in the B/S.

Let us consider two common types of off-balance-sheet financing devices:

- leasing

- quasi-subsidiaries.

LEASING

In Hong Kong, SSAP 14 *Leases* was issued by the HKICPA in October 1987 (revised February 2000), effective for accounting periods starting on or after 1 July 2000. In the UK, SSAP 21 *Accounting for Leases and Hire Purchase Agreement* was issued by the ASB (ASC) in August 1984 (amended February 1997), effective for accounting periods starting on or after 1 July 1984.

A 'lease' is defined as an agreement whereby the lessor conveys to the lessee in return for a payment or series of payments the right to use an asset for an agreed period of time.[11] In essence, a lease is a contract between lessees for the hire of a specific asset.[12] The lessor retains ownership of the asset but conveys the right of the use of the asset to the lessee for an agreed period of time in return for payment of specified rentals.[13] The term 'lease' also applies to other arrangements in which one party retains ownership of an asset but conveys the right to the use of the asset to another party for an agreed period of time in return for specified payments.

Leases can be classified as either operating leases or finance leases.[14] A finance lease is one that transfers substantially all the risks and rewards associated with ownership of an asset to the lessee. Title may or may not eventually be transferred. An operating lease is any lease other than a finance lease. The risks of ownership of an asset include the possibilities of losses from idle capacity, poor demand or technological obsolescence. On the other hand, the rewards of ownership include the profits deriving from the use of the asset, the appreciation in value and the residual value upon disposal (the benefits of the residual value depend on whether the title is transferred to the lessee at the end of the lease).

Classification of leases is important because it directly affects the accounting treatment.[15] To reflect the substance of a finance lease, it is more appropriate for the lessee to recognize both the leased asset and the corresponding lease obligations in its B/S. Similarly, the substance of the transaction is that the lessor has disposed of the rights associated with ownership in return for a stream of lease payment receipts. Therefore, instead of carrying the asset under its original classification (which may well be property, plant and equipment), the lessor should recognize the asset held under a finance lease as a receivable in the B/S. Lease payments receivable are treated by the lessor as a combination of repayments of principal and interest income.

Compliance with SSAP 14 of the HKICPA and SSAP 21 of the ASB ensure compliance with IAS 17 *Accounting for Leases* in all material aspects. There are no significant differences amongst the three standards.

QUASI-SUBSIDIARIES (OR NON-SUBSIDIARY-DEPENDENT ENTITIES)

In general, a group comprises a parent (holding company) and all its subsidiaries. It is a result of a business combination that exists when there are two or more organizations that act as an economic entity controlled by a common management. A business combination may be created by a takeover, an acquisition, a merger or a group reconstruction. In Hong Kong (the Companies Ordinance) and the UK (the Companies Act 1985 as amended by the Companies Act 1989), the legislations on the accounting for groups are similar. It provides that consolidated accounts or group accounts are to be prepared by the management of the acquirer and presented to the shareholders of the acquirer. Such consolidated accounts are required to present a true and fair view of the combined profit (loss) of the entity and of the combined assets and liabilities at the end of the year.

In order that the consolidated financial statements present financial information about the group as that of a single economic entity, the consolidation process involves:

- combining the financial statements of the parent and its subsidiaries line by line, by adding together like items of assets, liabilities, capital, revenues and expenses; and

- making certain consolidation adjustments.

The consolidation adjustments required vary with different circumstances. Examples of typical adjustments include:

- eliminating the carrying amount of the parent's investments in each subsidiary and the parent's portion of equity of each subsidiary;

- eliminating all intra-group balances and transactions and resulting unrealized profits or losses, including dividend received;

- making any adjustments for the purpose of standardizing accounting policies between entities in the group;

- adjusting for profit or loss arising from the disposal or partial disposal of interests in subsidiaries during the financial year; and

- identifying minority interests in profit or loss, and the net assets of consolidated subsidiaries (when a parent does not hold all the interest in a subsidiary, the capital of the subsidiary is allocated between the parent's interest and minority interest).

In Hong Kong, the HKICPA issued SSAP 32 *Consolidated Financial Statements and Accounting for Investments in Subsidiaries* in January 2001, effective for accounting periods starting on or after 1 January 2001. An organization should be consolidated when the substance of its relationship with the parent entity indicates that the organization is controlled by the parent entity (or the group). Sometimes, an entity may be created to accomplish a narrow and well-defined objective (for example, to effect a lease, research and development activities or a securitization of financial assets). Such a special purpose entity (SPE) may take the form of a corporation, trust, partnership or unincorporated entity.

In the UK, FRS 5 *Reporting the Substance of Transactions* was issued by the ASB in April 1994 (revised December 1994 and September 1998). FRS 5 defines a quasi-subsidiary (or a non-subsidiary dependent entity) of an organization as a company, trust, partnership or other vehicle that, though not fulfilling the definition of a subsidiary, is directly or indirectly controlled by the organization under report and gives rise to benefits that are in substance no different from those that would arise were the vehicle a subsidiary. Control of a subsidiary or quasi-subsidiary refers to the ability to direct the financial and operating policies of that entity with a view to gaining economic benefits from its activities.

Factors to consider in deciding whether an entity is a quasi-subsidiary are:

- whether the organization is the beneficiary of the entity's net assets, and exposed to the inherent risks;

- whether the organization directs the entity's financial and operating policies, and can prevent others from doing so;

- where the entity's financial and operating policies are in substance predetermined; then the organization possessing control is the beneficiary of the net assets.

The quasi-subsidiary should be included (consolidated) in the group financial statements as though it were a subsidiary. The fact of such inclusion should be disclosed in the Notes which summarize the financial statements of each quasi-subsidiary or group of similar quasi-subsidiaries.

In essence, the principle of consolidation is that all the entities under the control of an organization should be consolidated into a single set of financial statements. Applying this principle means that the assets, liabilities, revenues, expenses and cash flows of any quasi-subsidiary should be included in the group financial statements (on a line-by-line basis) in the same way as if they were those of a member of the statutory group.

Accounting irregularities of this kind may refer to the fact that assets and, predominantly, liabilities of a group are transferred to a quasi-subsidiary. Rather than a line-by-line consolidation, the net investment in the quasi-subsidiary is disclosed in the group's B/S in one line as investment. That is a way to strengthen the group's B/S because perpetrators believe that the gearing ratio is important.

Let us consider a relevant case.

CASE 6.3

CONSOLIDATION VS NET INVESTMENT

P Holding is the parent of a group with one wholly owned subsidiary (A Ltd) and one 60%-owned quasi-subsidiary (Q Ltd). Q Ltd has not yet commenced its business. At the financial year-end, P Holding's consolidated B/S is extracted as in Table 6.1.

Table 6.1   Regular consolidated B/S

	P Holding	A Ltd	Q Ltd	Consolidation adjustment Dr/(Cr)	Group
	$	$	$	$	$
Fixed assets	11 200	5 000	9 200	0	25 400
Investment in A Ltd	6 500	0	0	(6 500)	0
Investment in Q Ltd	3 000	0	0	(3 000)	0
Net current assets	1 450	1 550	1 800	0	4 800
Loan	(150)	(50)	(6 000)	0	(6 200)
	22 000	6 500	5 000	(9 500)	24 000
Capital	10 000	4 300	5 000	9 300	10 000
Reserve and profits	12 000	2 200	0	2 200	12 000
Minority interest (40% of Q Ltd's net assets) – note 1	0	0	0	(2 000)	2 000
	22 000	6 500	5 000	9 500	24 000

Note 1: $5000 × 40% = $2000

The group's existing gearing ratio is 25.8% ($6200 ÷ $24 000). However, the management of P Holding is concerned with the possible impact of Q Ltd's loan on the consolidated financial position. By manipulating with the arrangement of Q Ltd, Q Ltd's financial results are not consolidated. Instead, Q Ltd is accounted for as a net investment in P Holding's B/S. As a result, an irregular consolidated B/S is produced for the group as shown in Table 6.2.

Table 6.2   Irregular consolidated B/S

	P Holding	A Ltd	Consolidation adjustment Dr/(Cr)	Group	Q Ltd
	$	$	$	$	$
Fixed assets	11 200	5 000		16 200	9 200
Investment in A Ltd	6 500	0	(6 500)	0	0
Investment in Q Ltd	3 000	0		3 000	0
Net current assets	1 450	1 550	0	3 000	1 800
Loan	(150)	(50)	0	(200)	(6 000)
	22 000	6 500	(6 500)	22 000	5 000
Capital	10 000	4 300	4 300	10 000	5 000
Reserve and profits	12 000	2 200	2 200	12 000	0
	22 000	6 500	6 500	22 000	5 000

Based on the irregular balance sheet, P Group's gearing ratio is less than 1% ($200 ÷ $22 000). The gearing ratio has improved from 25.8% to 1% as a result of this irregularity.

A subsidiary should be excluded from consolidation when:[16]

- control by the parent is intended to be temporary because the subsidiary is acquired and held exclusively with a view to its subsequent disposal in the near future; or

- it operates under severe long-term restrictions which significantly impair its ability to transfer funds to the parent.

In the UK, companies' legislation and FRS 2 *Accounting for Subsidiary Undertakings* issued by the ASB require subsidiaries to be excluded from consolidation in certain circumstances. The most common reason (which is not allowed by SSAP 32 of the HKICPA) to justify non-consolidation is dissimilar activities. A highly leveraged group can benefit from such a scheme by improving its liquidity and solvency ratios.

However, while including a quasi-subsidiary in group financial statements is required in order that those financial statements give a true and fair view of the group, these exclusions may not be applicable to a quasi-subsidiary. The following considerations are relevant.[17]

- An immaterial quasi-subsidiary may be excluded from consolidation because GAAP need not be applied to immaterial items. It is particularly the case when disproportionate expense or undue delay is required in obtaining the relevant information for consolidation.

- The organization does not necessarily have the control fitting the definition of a quasi-subsidiary where there are severe long-term restrictions over the exercise of the organization's rights.

- Where there are significant differences between the activities of a quasi-subsidiary and those of the group that controls it, these should be disclosed. However, the quasi-subsidiary should nevertheless be included in the consolidation in order that the group financial statements present a true picture of the extent of the group's activities.

- It is appropriate to exclude a quasi-subsidiary from consolidation only where the interest in the quasi-subsidiary is held exclusively with a view to subsequent resale and the quasi-subsidiary has not previously been included in the organization's consolidated financial statements.

Compliance with SSAP 32 of the HKICPA and FRS 2 of the ASB ensure compliance with IAS 27 *Consolidated Financial Statements and Accounting for Investments in Subsidiaries* in many significant aspects. However, it is important to note that, unlike FRS 2 of the ASB, IAS 27 and SSAP 32 of the HKICPA do not have an exclusion from consolidation for a subsidiary based on the grounds that its activities are dissimilar from those of the group.

CONCLUSION

Liabilities play an important role in the calculation of an organization's net assets. Since liabilities are a deduction from assets, recording lower liabilities may inflate its net worth.

Learning from experience, organizations should stay alert to certain warning signs of possible accounting irregularities in the understatement of liabilities. To end this chapter, typical warning signs are set out for reference:

- weak cash flows from operations to service the concealed liabilities despite growing sales and profits;

- significant estimates on accruals and provisions involving subjective judgements or uncertainties that are difficult to explain and substantiate;

- excessive degree of participation or influence in the selection of accounting methods or the determination of significant estimates on accruals and provisions by management untrained in accounting and finance;

- abnormally high profit margins, possibly topping the industry league;

- allowance for sales returns, warranty claims, and so on that are declining in percentage terms, and possibly out of line with the industry norm;

- reducing trade creditors (both in numbers and individual balances) while the industry norm shows a lengthening payment cycle;

- significant transactions with related parties or special purpose entities not in the ordinary course of business or where those entities are unaudited or audited by a different auditor;

- unusual or highly complex transactions with limited substance and unclear beneficial ownership, especially those close to financial year-end;

- unexplained decrease in the level of purchases, trade creditors and creditor turnover ratios;

- gaps in the sequence of important documents, such as payment records and suppliers' invoices;

- gaps in the filing sequence of legal documents, such as solicitors' fee notes and other correspondence; and

- missing originals of important documents, such as legal correspondence, suppliers' contracts and title deeds.

Notes

1 – The HKICPA, *Framework for the Preparation and Presentation of Financial Statements,* issued in June 1997 and revised in May 2003

1, 5, 6, 7, 10 – SSAP 28 *Provisions, Contingent Liabilities and Contingent Assets* (issued by the HKICPA in January 2001, effective for accounting periods starting on or after 1 January 2001)

2, 3, 4, 6, 7, 10 – FRS 12 *Provisions, Contingent Liabilities and Contingent Assets* (issued by the ASB in December 1999, effective for accounting periods ending on or after 23 March 1999)

8, 9 – SSAP 34 *Employee Benefits* (issued by the HKICPA in May 2003, effective for accounting periods starting on or after 1 January 2002)

11, 14, 15 – SSAP 14 *Leases* (issued by the HKICPA in October 1987, revised February 2000, effective for accounting periods starting on or after 1 July 2000)

12, 13 – SSAP 21 *Accounting for Leases and Hire Purchase Agreement* (issued by the ASB [predecessor of the ASC] in August 1984, amended February 1997, effective for accounting periods starting on or after 1 July 1984)

16 – SSAP 32 *Consolidated Financial Statements and Accounting for Investments in Subsidiaries* (issued by the HKICPA in January 2001, effective for accounting periods starting on or after 1 January 2001)

17 – FRS 5 *Substance of Transactions* (issued by the ASB in April 1994, amended December 1994 and September 1998, effective for accounting periods ending on or after 22 September 1994)

CHAPTER 7

Presenting It Better

MANIPULATION OF CLASSIFICATION AND DISCLOSURE

'Presenting it better' is what drives some perpetrators. Classifying an item, disclosing a transaction or naming an account in an organization's financial statements can be as significant as the appropriate recognition and measurement of items and transactions. Readers' perception of an organization's performance may well hinge on how various line items, headings, sub-totals, descriptions and further analyses are presented and disclosed in the financial statements.

Processing and organizing large quantities of transactions and categorizing and aggregating into them into accounts according to their nature or function are the essence of financial statements. Revenue could be irregularly manipulated, as could assets; while expenditure and liabilities could be irregularly mis-stated. These kinds of accounting irregularities are discussed in the last four chapters and in Chapter 8, especially wherein the perpetrators described tend to make up fictitious transactions, falsify supporting documentations, conceal genuine items or change existing identities. In this chapter, we mainly consider accounting irregularities involving the manipulation of classification and disclosure of data presented in an organization's financial statements.

Classification refers to the process of arranging names and categories of accounts or line items for presentation in an organization's financial statements. Disclosure refers to the process of describing and presenting events, transactions and accounts in an organization's financial statements.

Defining the correct classification and disclosure in an organization's financial statements should be done with reference to the appropriate generally accepted accounting principles (GAAP). Any departure from these are deemed to be irregular (accounting irregularities). Relevant legislations in this context primarily refer to the Companies Ordinance in Hong Kong and the Companies Act in the UK.

Most accounting irregularities of this kind affect:

- the profit and loss account (P&L)
- the balance sheet (B/S)
- Notes to the financial statements (Notes).

Most organizations try to distinguish between the gross profit earned on trading, and a net profit after other revenues and expenses. The P&L is arguably the most significant single indicator of an organization's success or failure. It is very important to ensure that it is not presented in such a way as to be misleading.

The B/S is like a 'snapshot' photograph, since it captures a static image of something which is dynamic and continually changing. Like any photograph, it can be taken from different angles and standpoints. Some readers of financial statements may perceive the B/S as an indication of what the business is worth at the financial year-end, given a set of assumptions that are largely detailed in the Notes. The B/S is important to an organization because it is often used to determine things such as:

- credit worthiness – the extent of credit and the degree of credibility that the organization can obtain;

- credit limit – how much money that the organization can borrow; and

- cost of funding – the interest rate that is chargeable on the organization's borrowings.

The Notes are descriptive in nature and form the largest part of the financial statements. The Notes are important because they show the accounting policies used in the preparation of the financial statements and help to show how all the numbers in the financial statements fit together. We have considered in Chapter 2 the importance of accounting policies in identifying accounting irregularities.

Classification and disclosure of financial information may be done either on the face of the P&L and B/S or in the Notes. If a line item is not individually material, it is aggregated with other items either on the face of the P&L and B/S or in the Notes. An item that is not sufficiently material to warrant separate presentation on the face of the P&L and B/S may nevertheless be sufficiently material that it should be presented separately in the Notes.

PRESENTATION OF PROFIT

Profit tends to be the single indicator attracting most attention. Manipulation of classification and disclosure involving profit mainly falls into three categories, which are:

- components of profits (gross profit, operating profit and net profit)

- nature of occurrence (one-off item vs recurring item, and discontinuing item)

- reserve accounting ('below-the-line' movement).

We now consider each of them in the following three sections.

COMPONENTS OF PROFIT

There is more than one profit figure in a typical organization's P&L, such as gross profit, operating profit and net profit (profit before taxation). These are effectively the sub-totals of an organization's total profit. In addition, there are other components in deriving at the profit figure, such as cost of sales, selling expenses and administrative expenses. Most accounting irregularities relating to components of profit find their ways into the P&L mainly through shifting individual items around in order to change the sub-totals within the P&L.

Operating profit and net profit are two of the figures need to be shown on the face of an organization's P&L.[1] Operating profit comprises items associated with an organization's operating activities and should be useful in judging its basic operating performance. However, gauging the operating profit is not strictly defined under GAAP and allows a considerable degree of flexibility.

In some cases, the definition of 'operations' is rather vague. Whether or not classifying an item, such as restructuring charges, asset impairments, investment-related gains, charges relating to mergers and acquisitions, gains/losses on disposal of assets/subsidiary, store closure/relocation costs, legal/litigation costs, litigation settlements, costs of abandoned acquisition and charges for purchased research/ development, as recurring is dependent on its frequency of appearance.

Let us consider a relevant case.

CASE 7.1

OPERATING PROFIT VS PROFIT BEFORE TAXATION

P Ltd makes a one-off investment gain of $2 million in 2004. Because of the one-off nature of the investment gain, it should be classified outside of operating profit. This can avoid an unreasonable expectation on the sustainability of operating profit. This of course assumes that readers of financial statements focus on operating profit as providing a good initial representation of sustainable earnings performance. Although it may still include some non-recurring items, operating profit may be viewed as a better indicator of sustainable earnings than sub-totals further down the P&L.

However, directors of P Ltd want to maximize the market expectation on an organization's profitability. By putting the gain as a component within operating profit, directors of P Ltd mislead the reader to believe that the gain can be achieved again as shown in Table 7.1.

Table 7.1   One-off gain

P Ltd: Extracts from profit and loss account for 2004

	Regular amount $ million	Irregular amount $ million
Operating profit	9	11
Gain from disposal of investment	2	0
Other expenditure	(6)	(6)
Net profit	5	5

Net profit is the same under the two different types of classification of the $2 million investment gain. In the regular classification, the operating profit is $9 million. However, the irregular classification gives a higher operating profit figure at $11 million giving a (wrongly) perceived impression of a higher (and sustainable) earning capability of P Ltd.

Similarly, moving expenses from cost of sales to selling, general and administrative expenses may fabricate an overstated figure of gross profits, even though there is no impact on operating profit or net profit.

Let us consider a relevant case.

CASE 7.2

IMPACT OF COST OF SALES ON GROSS PROFIT

P Ltd records $50 million of sales for 2004. The cost of sales is $35 million, but P Ltd's management wants to portray good profitability. An accounting irregularity to boost the gross profit margin is committed by shifting $5 million of inward transportation cost from cost of sales to distribution costs after the gross profit.

Table 7.2   Shifting costs

P Ltd: Extracts from profit and loss account for 2004

	Regular amount $ million	Irregular amount $ million
Sales	50	50
Cost of sales	(35)	(30)
Gross profit	15	20
Distribution costs	(7)	(12)
Administrative expenses	(5)	(5)
Net profit	3	3
Gross profit margin	30%	40%
Net profit margin	6%	6%

> P Ltd recorded $5 million of cost of sales as distribution expenses and inflated the gross profit margin from 30% to 40%, even though the net profit and its margin remain the same at $3 million and 6% respectively.

An organization's expenses should be analysed and presented in the financial statements (preferably on the face of the P&L).[2] There are two bases for the analysis of expenses – nature of expenses and function of expenses.

For the 'nature of expenses' method, expenses are aggregated in the P&L according to their nature (for example, advertising, depreciation, purchases of materials, transportation, and wages and salaries), and are not reallocated amongst various functions within the organization. The 'function of expenses' method classifies expenses according to their function as part of cost of sales, selling, distribution or administrative activities. If an organization classifies expenses by function, it still has to disclose additional information on the nature of expenses by function, including depreciation charges and staff costs.

Both methods provide an indication of those costs which might be expected to vary with the organization's activity level. Choosing the most appropriate method requires consideration of:

- the history of the organization
- the industry norm
- the nature of the organization.

Because each method of presentation has its merit for different types of organization,[3] a choice needs to be made between classifications based on those that most fairly present the elements of the organization's performance.

Regardless of which method is chosen, perpetrators may try shifting expenses from cost of sales to administrative expenses, producing an irregular figure of inflated gross profits (no effect on operating profit and net profit). Alternatively, moving expenses from administrative expenses to cost of sales understates the gross profit figure (still no effect on operating profit and net profit).

Let us consider a relevant case.

CASE 7.3

COST OF SALES VS ADMINISTRATIVE AND OTHER EXPENSES

P Group is a property conglomerate in Hong Kong having subsidiaries engaged in property development, property investment and property trading. P Group classifies expenses by function and presents the expense headings on the face of its P&L for 2004.

Although there is no 'correct' classification as such because of the degree of judgement involved, it is important that the classification is consistently followed once adopted. Mr P (the Managing Director of P Group) is caught by committing the following irregular classifications:

- Mr P misclassifies loss on the sale of trading properties as an exceptional item after operating profit. However, it is irregular because the trading of properties is one of the principal activities of P Group. The loss should be analysed between turnover and cost of sales rather than disclosed as a single line item at a net amount of losses.

- Mr P misclassifies loss on the sale of investment properties as cost of sales. However, it is irregular because the sale of investment properties is not a principal activity of P Group. The loss should be included in other operating expenses (or regarded as a separate line item if the amount is material).

- Mr P misclassifies the Financial Controller's salary as cost of sales. However, it is irregular because this item forms part of the staff costs under administrative expenses, which should be separately disclosed.

- Mr P misclassifies a marketing person's salary as cost of sales. However, it is irregular because this item should be included under selling and distribution costs and forms part of the staff costs, which should be separately disclosed.

- Mr P misclassifies directors' emoluments as cost of sales. However, it is irregular because directors' emoluments are generally classified under administrative expenses. In some cases, if the directors are remunerated for certain specific functions, they should be included in that function (for example, salaries payable to the Marketing Director may be included in distribution costs).

- Mr P misclassifies interest expenses as net interest expense after offsetting with interest income. However, it is irregular because interest income should not generally offset against interest expenses. As financing business is not a principal activity of P Group, interest income should be included under the investment income or other revenue. Interest charges should be included under the finance cost heading.

NATURE OF OCCURRENCE

As a general rule for the P&L, all items of revenue and expense earned or incurred in a financial year should be included in the determination of the net profit or loss for that year unless the GAAP require otherwise. The net profit or loss comprises:[4]

- profit or loss from ordinary activities

- extraordinary items.

The two components should be disclosed on the face of the P&L.

Ordinary activities are defined as any activities which are undertaken by an organization as part of its business[5] and may include infrequent and unusual events.[6] Extraordinary items refer to revenue and expenses that arise from events or transactions that are clearly distinct from the organization's ordinary activities and therefore are not expected to recur frequently or regularly,[7] such as an earthquake or nationalization of the organization's assets. The nature and amount of each extraordinary item should be separately disclosed.

In the UK, the distinction between ordinary activities and extraordinary activities is more comprehensive. The ASB issued FRS 3 *Reporting Financial Performance* in October 1992 (amended in June 1993 and June 1999), effective from accounting periods ending on or after 22 June 1993. FRS 3 introduces a new format for the P&L, splitting continuing and discontinued operations. The definitions of these terms attempt to prevent manipulation. FRS 3 discloses more information and reflects the ASB's aim to avoid over-emphasis of any single accounting measurement in the financial statements.

All statutory headings from turnover to operating profit are subdivided between continuing and discontinued operations.[8] Turnover and operating profit are required to be fully analysed between existing operations and newly acquired operations. The results of the discontinued operation up to the termination date or the financial year-end date should be shown under each of the relevant P&L account headings.[9]

Once a business is committed to the disposal of an operation, all direct costs of termination and any operating losses up to the date of termination should be separately identified in the financial statements. Therefore, a question on the nature of occurrence can influence the trend or pattern of individual items or sub-totals in the P&L. It is therefore important to question revenues and expenditure in light of ordinary vs extraordinary and continuing vs discontinuing.

When there are gains, the perpetrators may move transactions out of the discontinued (or extraordinary) classification to continuing (or ordinary) operations. On the other hand, perpetrators may move transactions from continuing (or extraordinary) classification into discontinued (or extraordinary) operations when there are losses producing a higher figure of profits from ordinary activities. It is particularly true that when revenues from continuing (or ordinary) operations are below target, a revenue item is more likely to be classified as from a continuing (or ordinary) source. Just the opposite is true if revenue from continuing (or ordinary) operations was above target level. This kind of malpractice is irregular because the perpetrators decide on the timing of the change of categorization depending on the outcome (the figures in the financial statements) they require.

RESERVE ACCOUNTING

Another category of manipulation of classification and disclosure involving profit is 'reserve accounting'. It refers to deducting expenditure from the retained profits balance (the organization's reserve) rather than the P&L of the current financial year. By hiding such expenditure items from the current P&L, a more favourable presentation of the year's results may be achieved. Only a detailed examination of the previous year's B/S and the relevant Notes can reveal that the figures in the reserves brought forward are manipulated.

By excluding the items in this way from the current P&L, perpetrators argue that the item might have arisen in a previous year without becoming apparent until the current financial year. It is really a charge against previous year's profits and would have appeared in an earlier year's P&L if the directors had been aware of it. It is often referred to as a prior year adjustment.[10]

In the UK, a statement of total recognized gains and losses (STRGL) must be provided.[11] The ASB's objective is to turn the attention away from particular numbers or indicators and to encourage users to make their own judgements about an organization's performance based on the information given. The STRGL cannot be hidden because it must be given equal prominence with the other primary statements. A good example showing the importance of the STRGL applies to organizations with foreign currency transactions. The size of the exchange movements going through reserves can be considerable and, although they are disclosed, they may not be highlighted. The really important figure here is that of total gains and losses for the financial year. This will probably be of great importance to all readers in the future, as much as the profit for the financial year.

It is possible to extend the STRGL to reconcile the movements in shareholders' funds. In Hong Kong, the HKICPA issued SSAP 1 *Presentation of Financial Statements* in March 1984 (revised May 1999, August 2001 and December 2001), effective for accounting periods on or after 1 January 2002. SSAP 1 of the HKICPA introduces that the statement of changes in equity (SCE) is a primary statement and should therefore be presented with the same prominence as the other primary statements, namely, P&L, B/S and cash flow statement.

As a minimum, the SCE should show:[12]

- the net profit or loss for the financial year;

- each item of revenue and expense (or gain/loss), which is recognized directly as a change in equity; and

- the accumulative effects of changes in accounting policy and fundamental errors dealt with by prior year adjustment.

The following changes in equity may be presented within the SCE or in the Notes:[13]

- capital transactions with owners and distributions to owners;

- the balance of accumulated profit or loss at the beginning of the financial year and at the financial year-end date, and the movements for the financial year; and

- a reconciliation between the carrying amount of each class of equity capital, share premium and each reserve at the beginning and the end of the financial year, separately disclosing each movement.

SSAP 1 of the HKICPA provides flexibility for presenting the movements in share capital, reserves and accumulated profit either within the SCE or in the Notes. Changes in an organization's equity between two financial year-ends reflect the increase or decrease in its net assets or wealth. Except for changes resulting from transactions with shareholders, such as dividends, capital contributions and new issues of shares, the overall change in equity represents the total gains and losses generated by the organization's activities during the financial year. Incorporating all gains and losses in assessing the changes in an organization's financial position between two financial year-ends is important. Indeed, a SCE disclosing the first three items above highlights an organization's total gains and losses, including those that are recognized directly in equity.

OTHER AREAS IN MANIPULATION OF CLASSIFICATION AND DISCLOSURE

In addition to those affecting profits as discussed in the last section, manipulation of classification and disclosure may relate to other matters, such as:

- novelty in terminology

- aggressive offsetting

- abuse of materiality concept

- misclassification of accounts.

NOVELTY IN TERMINOLOGY

It is human nature to put the best face on adversity. During the last recession, it was common for organizations to use the term restructuring and to group every possible negative event together under this label. A positive market reaction is not surprising if it is assumed that the announcement is new to the market and that the restructuring shows the promise of an improving performance.

However, some organizations overdo it by bringing a wide range of costs under the restructuring umbrella (in some extreme cases, even future operating costs are included in restructuring costs). Positive labels are applied in cases that simply represent a clean-up activity resulting from bad commercial decisions. Substantial charges which surprise the readers without a reason or detailed plan are unlikely to be positive for the market. Readers of financial statements should try to ignore the labels and examine the character of the underlying charges and the associated activities.

Most people on this planet understand the importance of cash which is liquid and most straightforward (unlike other types of assets which require explanations and valuations). Therefore, many readers of financial statements believe (or are led to believe) that a charge is not as bad as it might have been if an immediate cash outflow is not required. Therefore, some perpetrators may characterize certain non-recurring charges as non-cash items with an undue emphasis. However, the actual cash outlay may take place in a financial year before the charge, during the year of the charge, or in years after the charge is recorded.

AGGRESSIVE OFFSETTING

As one of the fundamental concepts discussed in Chapter 2, assets and liabilities should not be offset unless offsetting is required or allowed by the GAAP. When an organization and another party owe each other certain amounts (as receivable or payable), the organization may be tempted to offset the two amounts in the B/S. Similarly, for revenue and expense arising from the same or similar transactions, the organization may wish to offset such amounts in the P&L.

However, offsetting means the loss of certain information, except when it is done to reflect the substance of the transactions or events. Otherwise, offsetting decreases transparency in the financial statements and denies the reader from understanding the transactions of events.

This offset reporting may increase the likelihood that important information is overlooked in assessing financial performance. The net balance of these various items is simply presented on the face of the P&L and the B/S. The Notes often are not identified with this line item. The best way for the readers of financial statements is to look for the detail of other revenue and expense notes, even in cases where the net balances are either small or relatively stable. It should be noted that presenting assets net of valuation allowances, such as provision for doubtful debts or inventory obsolescence, is not considered as offsetting.

UK GAAP recognizes the four fundamental accounting concepts of going-concern, prudence, accruals and consistency, describing them as accounting principles, along with a fifth principle, known as separate valuation. The separate-valuation principle states that, in determining the amount to be attributed to an asset or liability in the B/S, each component item of the asset or liability must be valued separately. These separate valuations are then totalled to arrive at the B/S figure. For example, if an organization's inventory comprises fifty separate items, each item should really be valued separately. Totalling the value of the fifty items gives the inventory figure in the financial statements.

How organizations report revenue for the goods and services they sell has become an increasingly important issue because the market may value certain organizations on a multiple of revenues rather than a multiple of profits. For example, sales and other revenues both increase if billings for shipping and handling are treated as part of sales revenue. To the extent that both sales and gross margin are key performance indicators, the perpetrators would be extremely concerned with the classification of certain items, such as shipping and handling costs. Gross margin can be improved if shipping and handling costs are pushed down into the selling, general and administrative expense category.

ABUSE OF MATERIALITY CONCEPT

As one of the fundamental concepts discussed in Chapter 2, materiality refers to the magnitude of a mis-statement, non-disclosure or misclassification of accounting information that is likely to change the judgement of a reasonable reader relying on that piece of information.

Materiality is the final test of what information should be given in a particular set of financial statements.[14] To maximize the usefulness of the financial information, the materiality test asks whether the resulting information content is of such significance as to require its inclusion in the financial statements.[15] Each material item should be presented separately in the financial statements. Immaterial amounts may be aggregated with amounts of a similar nature or function and need not be presented separately.

As a matter of adopted practice and conventional wisdom, any mis-statement or omission of an item that falls under a 5 per cent threshold is not material in the normal circumstances. However, this 5 per cent threshold rule of thumb is only an initial step in assessing materiality and cannot be used as a substitute for a full analysis of all relevant circumstances.

It is important to consider both the nature and amount of the item in question, that is, both quantitative and qualitative factors. Generally, an item is considered material if its mis-statement, non-disclosure or misclassification would mislead readers of the financial statements, such as the non-disclosure of a legal claim by one of the organization's major customers.

In considering whether an item is material, the following benchmarks should be checked:

- The amount of an item relating to B/S (and P&L in most cases) ought to be compared with the lower of:
  - net assets (difference between the organization's assets and liabilities); and
  - the total of the appropriate asset or liability class.

- In most kinds of organizations, the amount of the item relating to P&L should be compared with the operating profit or loss (or net profit or loss) for the current financial year (or an average over a number of years).

- In some cases when the organizations operate at or close to a break-even level, the amount of an item relating to the P&L ought to be compared with the appropriate revenue or expense amount for the current financial year (or an average over a number of years). Functioning at the break-even level means that the organization's results fluctuate between profits and losses from year to year, and any resulting profit or loss tends to be very small in size compared with the scale of the organization's operations.

Some perpetrators may use the materiality concept as an excuse for not correcting or disclosing certain errors or mis-statements. Manipulating the concept of materiality may lower the prominence of selected items in order to achieve a desired outcome in the P&L. Depending on the perpetrators' motive, it is also used as the basis for failing to disclose a so-called immaterial item of non-recurring revenue, gain, expense or loss.

Unlike other types of manipulation of classification and disclosure, the abuse of materiality may mean the disappearance of the item in question, that is the perpetrators may argue to remove 'immaterial' items away from the financial statements. Therefore, there is no way to find out how a reader, being provided with the detail, may react to the information.

MISCLASSIFICATION OF ACCOUNTS

The way of classifying an item in the financial statements (or in the underlying accounting ledgers) can directly affect its measurement and reported value. Classification of investments may itself change the carrying value. GAAP in Hong Kong and the UK allow the use of management judgement in the classification of investments into trading (short-term) or held-to-maturity (long-term) categories. Classification is to be made at the time of acquisition but can be changed subsequently, and the appropriateness of classifications made is to be reassessed at each financial year-end.

For businesses in trusts or investment funds, trading assets are generally valued at the market price (or so-called marked to market), while long-term investments are stated at their original costs less any permanent diminution in value. Trading investments are marked to market with resulting gains and losses reflected in the P&L. Investments held to maturity allow postponement of recognition in the retained profit (reserve) of any temporary decline in value. If the underlying investment has risen in value, misclassifying long-term investments as trading investments can bring forward unrealized marked to market gains – an overstatement in revenues and investments. On the contrary, misclassifying trading assets as long-term investments can postpone the decline in value until the time of disposal.

Another example of accounting irregularities involving misclassification of accounts are research and development expenditure. R&D is seen to form a crucial quantitative element of prospects and investment plans. Future prospects and investment for the future are often cited as what readers really want to see in financial statements. Organizations which develop computer software often express concerns over the impact of a high level of write-offs of R&D on their profits. Such costs are written off because they are often incurred on speculative software which are risky and may never be produced commercially. Therefore, some perpetrators may try misclassifying expenses falling in the category of R&D.

The misclassification in question may take place in the underlying accounting ledgers. Let us consider a relevant case.

CASE 7.4

BEAN-COUNTING AND INCORRECT VALUATION

P Ltd is engaged in the trading of soyabeans and holds a large volume of inventory at the financial year-end in 2004. P Ltd's inventory of soyabeans is bought through three different batches (at different prices). Set out in Table 7.3 is a summary of costs and net realizable value of each of the three batches of soyabean held by P Ltd.

Table 7.3   Misclassification of inventory

Inventory of soyabeans held by P Ltd at 31 December 2004

		Unit cost per bushel	Net realizable value per bushel (estimate)	Estimated profit/(loss) per bushel
		$		$
Inventory	Batch A	5.50	5.90	0.40
	Batch B	6.00	5.90	(0.10)
	Batch C	5.70	5.90	0.20

The appearance of all three batches of soyabeans look very similar, and it is easy to make an error in distinguishing them. Inventories from Batches A and C do not require any provisions and are stated at their costs. However, the net realizable value of Batch B is below its cost. By misclassifying soyabeans from Batch B to Batch A in the accounting ledgers, P Ltd avoids a provision of $0.10 per bushel. P Ltd has 5 million bushels of soyabeans from Batch B at 31 December 2004, and its inventories are overstated by $500 000 (= 5 000 000 x $0.10). By avoiding a provision, P Ltd's profit is also inflated by the same amount.

CONCLUSION

Accounting irregularities can happen in all directions with different intents. How an irregular act is committed depends on what the perpetrators want to achieve.

Learning from experience, organizations should stay alert to certain warning signs of possible accounting irregularities as set out in this chapter. To end this chapter, typical warning signs are set out for reference:

- sudden changes in the financial statements by comparison with the organization's historical average and/or the industry benchmark;

- significant transactions with related parties or other entities not in the ordinary course of business or where those entities are unaudited or audited by a different auditor;

- unusual or highly complex transactions whose substance and ownership is not known, especially those close to the financial year-end;

- unusual pattern of performance and financial situation recorded only in certain business units that are not shared by other parts of the same organization;

- gaps in the sequence of important documents, such as contracts, certificates, confirmations, invoices, delivery notes and title deeds;

- missing originals of important documents, such as contracts, certificates, confirmations, invoices and title deeds.

Notes

1 – The Companies Ordinance, Hong Kong
  – The Companies Act, UK
1, 2, 3, 12, 13, 15 – SSAP 1 *Presentation of Financial Statements* (issued by the HKICPA in March 1984, revised May 1999, August 2001 and December 2001, effective for accounting periods starting on or after 1 January 2002)
1, 4, 6, 8, 9, 10, 11 – FRS 3 *Reporting Financial Performance* (issued by the ASB in October 1992, amended June 1993 and June 1999, effective for accounting periods ending on or after 22 June 1993)
4, 5, 7, 10 – SSAP 2 *Net Profit or Loss for the Period, Fundamental Errors and Changes in Accounting Policies* (issued by the HKICPA in March 1984, revised December 1993 and May 1999 and October 2001, effective for accounting periods starting on or after 1 January 1999)
14 – The ASB, *Statement of Principles for Financial Reporting*, issued in December 1999

CHAPTER 8

Other Types of Accounting Irregularities

We have already considered the main categories of accounting irregularities in the last five chapters:

- overstatement of sales revenue
- understatement of expenditure
- overstatement of assets
- understatement of liabilities
- manipulation of classification and disclosure.

These accounting irregularities tend to occur more often and attract most of the media's attention due to the higher monetary value at stake. As driven by perpetrators' motives, the purposes of these accounting irregularities are to create a distorted picture of an organization's financial health so that an organization might appear to:

- have sold more than it has;
- have spent less than it has;
- own more than it possesses;
- owe less than it is obliged to pay.

It is important to bear in mind that there are other malpractices, such as:

- understatement of sales revenue
- overstatement of expenditure
- understatement of assets
- overstatement of liabilities
- keeping questionable transactions off the accounting books and records (off-book fraud, which is similar to off-book expenditure as in Chapter 4).

In general, these accounting irregularities try to portray a different image from what we have considered in the last five chapters. The reason is obvious because the perpetrators in question are being driven by different intents. In most cases, stealing from an organization (embezzlement) or the understatement of an organization's profitability and/or net worth are what the perpetrators try to accomplish.

Let us consider these tricks and some relevant cases in the context of four scenarios of intents:

- Tax evasion
- Theft
- Commercial disputes
- Matrimonial breakdown.

It is important to bear in mind that not all the perpetrators' tricks set out in this chapter relate to accounting. However, they are all irregular acts concerned with accounting documentation and records and having an ultimate impact on an organization's financial statements.

TAX EVASION

If a perpetrator is the proprietor of his or her business, tax evasion is an obvious motive to commit accounting irregularities – whether it is the skimming of sales revenue or whether it is a matter of fiddling with expenses for personal uses. The perpetrator wants to pay less tax than is required by law. Manipulating the organization's financial statements, making it show a lower amount of taxable profit or a higher amount of loss, can certainly help to achieve the perpetrator's intent.

Let us consider two cases involving tax evasion.

CASE 8.1

A DOCTOR'S UNDECLARED REVENUES

Dr P is one of the directors of a national chain of health care clinics. Dr P requests most patients pay in cash. Dr P's accounting records show the specific dates on which a particular patient is examined and pays for the medication. Those records are reflected and reconciled to the cash books (receipts), patient cards and patient ledgers. Due to patient confidentiality and medical jargon, Dr P's accounting records contain many abbreviations and codified messages.

To take advantage of this practice, Dr P uses dots and dashes as his own notations of accounting irregularities. At first glance, these dots and dashes appear to be natural without any implication. However, upon further analyses, it becomes apparent that Dr P uses a dot representing $1000 and a dash for $2000 of hidden receipts, that is, additional receipts over what is recorded in the accounting records.

Traditional auditing techniques such as analyses of patients' records or appointment books are unable to determine whether cash is being deposited. The auditor looks beyond the surface, uncovering the cash position of Dr P's medical practice, and pieces together Dr P's personal and other business transaction cash flows. From the known businesses to Dr P's personal bank accounts, relevant cash flows are traced in the form of drawing, salary and expense allowance. Time and amounts of deposits and their frequencies are correlated to establish a pattern and trend.

Reviewing Dr P's personal bank accounts is extremely important because personal bank accounts reveal normal living expenses, such as food, clothing, utilities, rent and transportation. There is no indication of diversion of cash out of the business for unrecorded personal purposes. However, there is a strong indication that a significant amount of revenue is unrecorded.

A perpetrator's own ego can often work against them, such that the perpetrator tends to keep a record of what the real revenue is, which can provide implicating evidence once in the auditor's hands. In this case, Dr P is caught by his own notations and records. If Dr P were not concerned about exactly how much he actually earns, he might not have been caught.

CASE 8.2

A LOSS-MAKING COLLEGE

Mr P runs a private college offering tuition classes mainly to adults in a variety of subjects. About half of his students pay in cash. The college's accounting records link students' enrolment forms with invoices. Most staff and teachers work part-time and are paid in cash.

Regardless of the introduction of new government initiatives of providing adult education grants, the college continuously suffers losses. Mr P indeed understates the declared revenues of the college. To collect evidence and to quantify the understated amount of revenues, the auditor (without revealing their identity) calls up the college and asks about the availability of tuition and the enrolment number of each class. On this basis and the available course brochures, the auditor reconstructs a profile of the college in terms of the number of students, the tuition rates of various classes and the gross revenues.

> An important point to note is that sometimes a simple matter such as a phone call can be extremely fruitful in investigation of this kind.

Many organizations offer their employees (or proprietors) the ability to use the corporate assets and goods in their personal lives. In most cases, the value is usually not material. However, when the amount becomes material, an adjustment may be necessary to remove non-business expenses from the profit and loss account to personal current accounts.

Similarly, a question is often asked as to whether the employees' wages and salaries exceed a reasonable level, to ensure that the payroll is what is necessary for the business and no more. Due to the differential in tax rates, it may be beneficial for some proprietors to manipulate the drawings from their business via salaries to themselves or their close relatives. Let us consider a case involving wages and salaries.

CASE 8.3

A WIFE'S JOB

This case involves Mr and Mrs P (husband and wife). Mrs P is employed as the Administration Manager by P Ltd which is under Mr P's ownership and control. However, Mrs P is in fact not required to be present at work, and she receives $35 000 a month for this employment. The auditor has found that her office in which she allegedly works is clearly an unused office because of the emptiness of that office and the surrounding dust; it is totally unused and has no personal effects. All this indicates a no-show job with significant compensation for Mrs P. Mr P manipulates the drawings from P Ltd via salaries to Mrs P in order to evade their tax liabilities.

Tax rates for individuals and organizations tend to be different in most parts of the world. The effective tax rate would depend on the situation of the individuals or organizations in question. Whenever the effective tax rate differential provides an incentive to do so, perpetrators may find a way to minimize their tax liability; sometimes it breaks the rules and becomes an accounting irregularity.

Whatever the intent might be, 'ghost employees' remain a common disputed item in tax evasion cases. The term basically refers to someone on the payroll who does not actually work for the organization in question. It is important to bear in mind that ghost employees might be created by employees (staff perpetrators, rather than the proprietors of an organization) so that cash and other valuable assets are stolen from the organization (see *Theft* section of this chapter).

Perhaps the classic example for personal expenses of a business nature being paid through an organization is entertaining and travelling. The relevant question to ask is whether these expenses are for advancing the business interest of the organization in question.

If financial statement readers would like to analyse this category of expenses, it is important to obtain the originals of the receipts. Most financial institutions (issuers of credit cards) nowadays give listings of the names of stores, restaurants or hotels that charge the expenses and their dates and amounts. However, some information on the originals may be missing, such as the signature of the person who signed for it and detailed breakdowns of a hotel bill which may show a personal purchase at the gift shop. It is not uncommon to find that the perpetrator's spouse has signed on a number of charge slips – a strong indication of the personal nature of the expenditure. Assessing the nature of entertaining and travelling expenses, whether in summaries provided by the financial institutions or individual charge slips, can indicate the extent that one may personally benefit from the business.

Another category of expenses commonly involving items of a personal nature is repairs and maintenance expenses. One cannot necessarily rely on vendor billing detail – some vendors might be prepared to give a business address on a bill rather than a personal address. In addition to household repair and maintenance work, one might find laundry and cleaning services being paid through the business. It is often difficult to determine the true nature of expenses unless the vendor gives accurate and honest detail on the billing. Both in Hong Kong and the UK, the relevant legislations allow expenses to be deducted from revenues in calculating the assessable profits only so long as those expenses are incurred wholly, necessarily and exclusively for the purpose of producing those revenues for the organization.

THEFT

Theft is the act of stealing or dishonestly misappropriating assets. We have considered theft in the context of the financial reporting environment in Chapter 1. In connection with accounting irregularities, theft may refer to the non-recording of legitimate transactions and their accounting entries. The impact is therefore an understatement of sales revenue and assets.

Let us consider three types of theft:

- ghost employees
- skimming of proceeds
- theft of assets.

GHOST EMPLOYEES

A 'ghost employee' may be created through the falsification of an organization's personnel or payroll records. In most cases, the perpetrator, usually with the help of an accomplice, makes pay cheques to themselves. The ghost employee may be a fictitious person or a genuine individual who simply does not work for the organization in question. When it is a real person, it is often a friend or relative of the perpetrator.

Under a proper system of internal control, every name on the payroll should be verified against personnel records to make sure that those persons receiving pay cheques actually work for the organization; but in practice this does not always happen. Thus, persons responsible for preparing an organization's payroll may be able to create fictitious employees by simply adding a new name to the payroll records. Access to these records is usually restricted to certain managerial staff. As these persons often have the ability to make changes to the payroll, they are likely to be the staff perpetrators in a ghost employees scheme. Let us consider a relevant case.

CASE 8.4

'GENUINE' EMPLOYEES

Mr P is a manager in an event and conference management organization, responsible for hiring and scheduling part-time workers in various duties for a series of events and conferences. Mr P is so trusted that the director tends not to check his work and payment requests before approval. The lack of separation of duties and the absence of proper review makes it simple for Mr P to add a fictitious employee into the payroll system. Mr P indeed adds over 30 'ghost employees' to his payroll.

The ghost employees are in fact genuine individuals who know Mr P and work freelance. Having completed time sheets for the 30 ghost employees and authorized them, Mr P takes the resulting pay cheques to the ghost employees, who cash them and split the proceeds with Mr P. It is in Mr P's authority to hire and supervise employees that enable him to fabricate this accounting irregularity. Mr P is caught as soon as the repeated overruns in staff costs are questioned.

Sometimes, perpetrators may create a ghost employee with a name very similar to that of a real employee. The name on the fraudulent pay cheques may appear to be legitimate to anyone who takes a quick glance at it. For example, if an organization has an employee named Jenny Chang, the ghost employee may be named Jenny Cheng.

Rather than adding new names, some perpetrators run ghost employee schemes by keeping the names of terminated employees on the payroll. Pay cheques to the terminated employee continue to be issued even though the employee no longer works for the organization in question. The perpetrator intercepts these fraudulent pay cheques and converts them for their own use.

Another common way of misappropriating funds from the payroll is the overpayment of wages. For hourly employees, the size of a pay cheque is based on two factors: the number of hours worked and the pay rate. An hourly staff perpetrator may fraudulently increase the size of their pay cheque, either by falsifying the number of hours worked or by changing their wage rate. For salaried employees whose pay is not based on their time at work, fraudulent wages may be produced by increasing their pay rate.

In reviewing accounting irregularities involving overstated hours, it is important to ascertain how an employee's time at work is recorded. There are three main ways:

- clock cards that employees insert into the clock at the beginning and end of work, and the time is imprinted on the card

- smart cards that track the time employees spend on the job based on their entries and exits at the office's main door or by a similar measure

- timesheets that employees complete showing the number of hours worked in a particular day, often prepared manually by the employee and approved by their manager.

Accordingly, perpetrators may obtain the appropriate approval by three irregular ways:

- forging a manager's signature

- collusion with a manager

- bypassing a manager's review (when a manager becomes overly trustful of certain employees, the dangers of rubber-stamping may emerge).

SKIMMING OF PROCEEDS

Cash is most vulnerable to theft (or skimming) because it is desirable, portable and indistinguishable. Skimming refers to the removal of cash from an organization before its entry into the double-entry book-keeping system. The audit trail is only at the minimal level because the stolen cash is never recorded and the organization's management may not be aware of the existence of the cash.

Skimming of proceeds may occur at any point where cash enters a business. Almost any member of staff who deals with the process of receiving cash may be in a position to perpetrate such an act, including salespersons, cashiers, waiters and others who receive cash directly from customers.

A classic example of skimming occurs when a salesperson sells goods or services to a customer and collects the customer's payment without making any record of the sale. The salesperson simply pockets the money received from the customer instead of turning it over to their employer. Similarly, skimming applies to cash or cheques coming through the mail. When receiving and logging payments made by customers through the mail, staff perpetrators (employees of the organization) may just skip the entries instead of posting the receipts to the proper revenue or receivables accounts.

The salesperson may also enter a void or other non-cash transaction to conceal the skimming of cash proceeds. The false transaction is entered in the till as a sale is being concluded. The staff perpetrator opens the till drawer and pretends to place the cash proceeds in the drawer. To customers and other members of staff in the store, it looks as though the sale is being properly recorded, but the cash proceeds are actually pocketed. The effects are not discovered until the weekly reconciliation of till roll to the cash in the till.

Another way to skim cash proceeds is to keep the store open and conduct sales during non-business hours, such as evenings, weekends or public holidays. As long as the staff perpetrators have the key to the store, they can gain access during those hours. The staff perpetrators can pocket the proceeds of all sales made during these times because the official records have no trace of those receipts and the management of the organization do not expect to have any sales during those non-business time-slots.

The above discussion focuses on purely *off-book fraud* – those which are never recorded. Accounting irregularities of understated sales are similar because the transactions in question are posted to the books, but for a lower amount than the perpetrator actually collects – the perpetrator skims the shortfalls. One way staff perpetrators commit understated sales schemes is by changing receipts or preparing falsified receipts that decrease the amount of sales. In a typical scheme, an employee enters a sales total which is lower than the amount actually paid by the customer. The employee skims the difference between the actual purchase price of the item and the sales figure recorded on the register.

Let us consider a relevant case.

CASE 8.5

SHORTFALLS OF RECORDED SALES

P Ltd sells $25 000 worth of goods to Customer A. An invoice is raised for $25 000 and is fully settled by Customer A. However, Mr P (owner of P Ltd) enters the sales as $20 000 and falsifies an invoice to reflect this understated amount. The cheque of $25 000 is received and deposited into P Ltd's secret bank account, and a corresponding cash deposit of $20 000 is entered into P Ltd's official bank account as settlement of the falsified invoice.

On the falsified invoice, perpetrators record the sale of fewer items. It is 25 units sold at $1000 each (= $25 000), but P Ltd only records the sale of 20 units at $1000 each (= $20 000) and skims the excess receipts of $5000 (= $25 000 − $20 000). P Ltd is caught when the auditor investigates the inventory shortfall. However, perpetrators may reduce the price from $1000 to $800 ($800 × 25 units = $20 000). This would have covered the inventory shortfall. Still, if the balance with Customer A is outstanding at a financial year-end, an audit confirmation should be able to reveal the $5000 difference.

Another example may well be that a staff perpetrator issues a cash receipt to a customer, but the carbon paper backing on the receipt is removed so that an official copy is not produced for the organization's records. The staff perpetrator then uses a pencil to prepare the official copy that shows a lower purchase price. The staff perpetrator skims the difference between the actual amount of revenue and the amount reflected on the fraudulent receipt.

Staff perpetrators with the authority to grant discounts may abuse their authority to skim sales and receivables. In a false-discount skimming scheme, a staff perpetrator accepts full payment for an item, but records the transaction as if the customer has a discount. The staff perpetrator skims the amount of the discount. A related scheme occurs when a staff perpetrator sells goods to an accomplice at an unauthorized discount.

THEFT OF ASSETS

Most thefts of an organization's assets are cash, but losses can be on other assets. Staff perpetrators may have access to an organization's assets in their daily work and can easily carry the assets away in front of other employees. When people see a trusted colleague removing items, most people assume that the staff perpetrator has a legitimate reason for doing so. In extreme cases, when senior managerial members of staff are stealing from their organizations, other employees often overlook the crime because they fear they may lose their jobs if they report it. Unfortunately, staff perpetrators who steal from their organizations are often highly trusted. Since they are trusted, they may be given access to restricted areas, lockers and deposit safes.

Asset requisitions and other documents that allow non-cash assets (valuable raw materials) to be moved from one location in an organization to another can be used to facilitate the theft of those assets. Staff perpetrators use internal transfer paperwork to gain access to assets which they otherwise might not be able to handle without raising suspicion. These documents do not account for missing assets the way false sales do, but they allow a person to move the assets from one location to another and the staff perpetrator simply steals the assets during the transition.

In some cases, a staff perpetrator may overstate the amount of supplies or equipment required to complete their work and steal the excess. In some aggressive schemes, the staff perpetrator even invents a completely fictitious project which legitimizes the use of certain assets they intend to steal.

Let us consider two relevant cases.

CASE 8.6

FRAUDULENT AUTHORIZATION

Mr P is one of the three shareholders of a computer consulting business, IT Ltd. Mr P uses false project documents to request $150 000 worth of computer chips, allegedly to upgrade IT Ltd's computers. Any purchase requisition above $100 000 from a shareholder requires a verbal confirmation from the other two shareholders. Mr P sets up an elaborate telephone scheme in order to get the project approved. Mr P uses his knowledge of IT Ltd's telephone system to divert calls from the other two shareholders' lines to his own desk. When the Buying Manager, who has recently joined IT Ltd and is unfamiliar with the shareholders personally, makes the confirmation call, it is diverted to Mr P who answers the phone and authorizes the project. Mr P then steals those computer chips from IT Ltd.

Fraudulent documents allow the employees to remove goods from the warehouse, but instead of using the goods for a work-related purpose, the perpetrator simply takes them home. Let us consider a relevant case.

CASE 8.7

STOLEN HANDSETS

Mr P is a Branch Manager of a telecommunication company (T Ltd) and requests a series of the latest mobile handsets for T Ltd's warehouse to be displayed in his showroom. The items requested by Mr P do not reach the showroom because he takes them home.

Mr P requests the handsets via computer using a management-level security code. The code is not specific to any particular manager, so there is no way of knowing which manager orders the handsets. Mr P is caught because T Ltd is able to record the computer terminal from which the request is made. Mr P uses his own computer to make the request, which leads to his arrest.

Staff perpetrators can also manipulate an organization's purchasing and receiving functions to facilitate the theft of inventories and other assets. If the inventories are misappropriated by the perpetrator, the organization loses both the value of the inventories and the use of the inventories. If someone is in charge of both the purchasing and receiving functions of the organization, they are in a position to falsify the records of incoming shipments. For example, if a staff perpetrator purchases and receives 10 000 units of a particular item and indicates that only 9000 are received, then by marking the shipment short, the staff perpetrator steals the 1000 units that are unaccounted for. However, the problem will surface when the receiving report does not match the vendor's invoice (the vendor bills for 10 000 units but the accounts payable voucher only shows receipt of 9000 units).

Sometimes, staff perpetrators try to avoid this problem by altering only one copy of the receiving report. The copy that is sent to accounts payable indicates receipt of a full shipment so that the vendor is paid without any questions. The copy used for inventory records indicates a short shipment so that the assets on hand equate the inventory records. However, the discrepancy between the accounts payable and the inventory records remains unresolved.

Instead of marking a shipment short, the staff perpetrator might reject portions of a shipment as being different from the specifications. The staff perpetrator then keeps the sub-standard goods rather than sending them back to the vendor. The result is the same as marking the shipment short. The fraud is discovered when the vendor chases up the sub-standard goods.

COMMERCIAL DISPUTES

Many merger and acquisition deals contain a deferred consideration, which is a payment based on the future performance of the business acquired, so-called 'earn-outs'. An earn-out clause means that the buyer makes an up-front payment, with further payments based on a multiple of future profits of the acquired business. Therefore, the new owner of the business has an incentive to suppress its profitability during the earn-out period and to minimize the amount payable to the previous owner of the business.

Including an earn-out clause in acquisitions has a number of advantages for the buyer of a business. It limits the downside risks. If the acquisition performs badly, the deferred consideration payments are adjusted downwards accordingly. In addition, there is often an immediate enhancement to earnings: the profits of the acquired organization are consolidated at once because the additional consideration is only paid some time later and it is often difficult to accrue for the deferred consideration with a high degree of certainty.

Commercial disputes also arise in existing businesses amongst shareholders and relate to a buy-out of one side's shareholdings on the basis of a business valuation. If the buyer is the management who has control over the financial statements, there exists a strong incentive to suppress the organization's profitability and net assets.

Contracts in the commercial world often involve a formula in calculating a monetary reward on the basis of figures in financial statements. Examples include the calculation of commissions on the basis of sales and the payment of interest on the basis of outstanding loan balances. Another type of commercial dispute relates to alleged breach of contracts. In cases involving sales commissions and under-reported sales, the claimants are entitled to recoup losses on the basis of the relevant contract terms. In assessing 'what-if' scenarios and quantum of losses (due to the alleged breach), claimants have the incentive to portray a depressed financial picture because the worse the claimants' financial health becomes the more the claim can be.

A trick of suppressing revenues and assets often used in commercial disputes is sometimes known as the 'cookie jar' reserve. It refers to an excessive level of accrual of operating expenses and the creation of liability accounts in order to absorb future years' operating expenses (those expenses which should have been charged in future years according to the generally accepted accounting principles). It involves the use of overly prudent assumptions in estimating liabilities. In essence, the practice entails reducing earnings during good years by stashing amounts in a cookie jar, then the organization reaches into the cookie jar in bad times.

Similarly, 'big bath' refers to a blanket write-off of assets and accrual of liabilities, usually in bad years, in order to make the balance sheet particularly conservative so that there are fewer expenses to serve as a drag on earnings in future years. Organizations use large restructuring charges to clean up their B/S, thus the term 'big bath'. The temptation is for organizations to overstate these charges because investors will look beyond the one-time loss and focus only on future earnings.

If some extra cushioning can be built into the charge that is taken, making it overly conservative, then the amount of that extra cushioning is credited as revenue in the P&L when estimates change or future earnings fall short. If organizations see that a large loss is inevitable, then they write off as large as amount as possible on the understanding that readers tend to be less concerned with the absolute amount of losses (because all losses are bad in the eyes of readers). Future financial statements are thus relieved from these losses and provide a boost to the organization's profits.

Commercial disputes can sometimes be tangled with matrimonial breakdown. Matrimonial breakdown often requires an assessment of the spouse's net worth. If the higher-paid spouse runs a business, their net worth may be checked to the organiz-ation's financial statements. There is a strong incentive for the higher-paid spouse to suppress the organization's profitability and net assets in order to reach a lower amount of maintenance settlement. Let us consider a case.

CASE 8.8

SUDDEN DROP IN SALARIES

Mr and Mrs P establish their own business (P Ltd) in 1999. Mr P is a director and the General Manager and receives $100 000 a month for this position from 1999 to 2003. However, all of a sudden, in 2004, Mr P's salary is reduced to $60 000 which coincides with a divorce action. Such a drop is not reasonable in light of P Ltd's rising volume and profitability. Such a situation may be indicative of careful divorce planning.

Mr P may be intentionally reducing his reported revenue for reasons relating to his divorce, such as a desire to minimize the perceived degree of his ability to support Mrs P (his soon-to-be ex-wife). Mr P's salary level is challenged by the auditor acting for Mrs P in assessing the amount of maintenance payment. The fictitious reduction in salary is treated as an accounting irregularity and is disregarded by the auditor as endorsed by the settlement judgement.

CONCLUSION

Accounting irregularities can happen in all directions with different intents. How an irregular act is committed depends on what the perpetrators want to achieve.

Perpetrators are less likely to strike if they have positive feelings about an organization than when they feel abused, threatened or ignored. Poor employee morale can affect an employee's attitude about committing accounting irregularities against an organization. Factors discouraging a positive environment and increasing the risk of accounting irregularities include:

- unreasonable budget expectations or other financial targets;
- top management that does not seem to care about or reward appropriate behaviour;
- negative feedback and lack of recognition for job performance;
- perceived inequality in the organization;
- lack of consultation and autocratic rather than participative management;
- rewards to employees at a below-the-market rate;
- poor training, promotion and career advancement opportunities;
- lack of clear organizational responsibilities;
- poor communication within the organization;
- allegation or investigation by regulators and other authorities;
- payment of fines or penalties imposed by the court or regulators;
- payments for unspecified services;
- unusual balance with consultants, related parties, employees or quasi-government bodies;
- sales commissions or agents' fees which are significantly different from the industry norm;
- transactions significantly different from the market rate;
- unusual payments in cash or cheques payable to bearer;
- unusual transactions with companies registered in tax havens;
- lack of adequate audit trail or sufficient evidence without reasonable explanations;

- unauthorized transactions or improperly recorded transactions; and

- negative media commentaries.

Employees can help create a positive environment and support the organization's values and code of conduct. They should have the opportunity to provide input to the development and updating of the organization's code of conduct, and to ensure that it is relevant, clear, fair and acceptable. We shall consider the deterrents to accounting irregularities in Chapter 9.

Deterrents to Accounting Irregularities

RESPONSIBILITIES

In a stewardship capacity, the one carrying the responsibility for the well-being of an item or event should do everything possible to protect the item from undue risk or danger. That is the basic requirement for a custodian in a fiduciary role. Therefore, in discussing the deterrents to accounting irregularities, it is appropriate to consider where the responsibilities might fall.

AUDITORS' RESPONSIBILITIES

Audit is a must for many limited companies in Hong Kong and the UK. Accordingly, there are regulations governing the audit and the auditing profession at large. In Hong Kong, the HKICPA has issued the Statements of Auditing Standards (SAS) for its members to follow. In the UK, the Auditing Practice Board (APB) published the Statements of Auditing Standards (SAS). SAS in Hong Kong and the UK both contain the basic principles and essential procedures with which auditors are required to comply. These regulations serve as a strong deterrent to accounting irregularities.

In planning an audit, performing the procedures, evaluating the results and reporting, the auditors should consider the risk of material mis-statements in the financial statements (largely defined in the same sense as accounting irregularities) resulting from error or fraud.[1]

Error refers to an unintentional mis-statement in financial statements, including the omission of an amount or a disclosure. Fraud refers to an intentional act by one or more individuals among management, those charged with governance, employees, or third parties, involving the use of deception to obtain an unjust or illegal advantage. Auditors' main concerns are on those fraudulent acts causing a material mis-statement in the financial statements. Mis-statements in financial statements are usually a means to an end rather than an end in itself and tend not to be the prime objective of some frauds.

Two types of intentional mis-statements are relevant to the auditors' consideration of fraud: mis-statements resulting from fraudulent financial reporting and mis-statements resulting from misappropriation of assets.[2]

Fraudulent financial reporting, which is a main type of accounting irregularity, involves intentional mis-statements or omissions of amounts or disclosures in financial statements to deceive their readers. Fraudulent financial reporting may involve:

- deception such as manipulation, falsification, or alteration of accounting records or supporting documents from which the financial statements are prepared;

- misrepresentation in, or intentional omission from, the financial statements of events, transactions or other significant information;

- intentional misapplication of accounting principles relating to measurement, recognition, classification, presentation or disclosure.

Misappropriation of assets can be accomplished in a variety of ways (including embezzling receipts, stealing physical assets or confidential data, or causing an organization to pay for goods and services not received). It is often accompanied by false or misleading records or documents in order to conceal the fact that the assets are missing, thereby indirectly causing accounting irregularities in financial statements.

The objective of an audit of financial statements is to enable the auditors to express an opinion whether the financial statements are prepared, in all material respects, in accordance with the generally accepted accounting principles. An audit conducted in accordance with SAS is designed to provide reasonable assurance that the financial statements taken as a whole are free from material mis-statement, whether caused by error or fraud. The fact that an audit is carried out may act as a deterrent, but the auditors are not and cannot be held responsible for the prevention of fraud and error.[3]

There are inherent limitations in an audit. There is an unavoidable risk that some material mis-statements of the financial statements may not be detected, even though the audit is properly planned and performed in accordance with SAS. An audit does not guarantee the detection of all material mis-statements because of such factors as the use of judgement, the use of sample testing, the inherent limitations of internal control and the fact that much of the evidence available to the auditors is persuasive rather than conclusive in nature. For these reasons, the auditors are able to obtain only reasonable assurance that material mis-statements in the financial statements will be detected.[4]

Fraud may involve sophisticated and carefully organized schemes designed to conceal it, such as forgery, deliberate failure to record transactions or intentional misrepresentations being made to the auditors. Such attempts at concealment may be even more difficult to detect when accompanied by collusion. Collusion may cause the auditors to believe that evidence is persuasive when it is, in fact, false.[5]

The risk of the auditors not detecting a material mis-statement resulting from frauds perpetrated by senior management is greater because those charged with governance and senior management are often in a position that assumes their integrity and enables them to override the formally established control procedures. Senior management may be in a position to override control procedures designed to prevent similar frauds by other employees and have the ability to either direct junior employees to do something or solicit their help to assist senior management in carrying out a fraud, with or without the employees' knowledge.[6]

The auditors' opinion on the financial statements is based on the concept of obtaining reasonable assurance; hence, in an audit, the auditors do not guarantee that material mis-statements, whether from error or fraud, will be detected.[7]

RESPONSIBILITIES OF THOSE CHARGED WITH GOVERNANCE AND OF MANAGEMENT

The primary responsibility for the prevention and detection of error and fraud rests with both those charged with governance and the management of an organization.[8] It is the responsibility of those charged with governance of an organization to ensure, by overseeing management, the integrity of an organization's accounting and financial reporting systems and that appropriate controls are in place, including those for monitoring risk, financial control and compliance with the law.

It is the responsibility of the management of an organization to establish a control environment and maintain policies and procedures to ensure, as far as possible, the orderly and efficient conduct of the organization's business.[9] This responsibility includes implementing and ensuring the continued operation of accounting and internal control systems which are designed to prevent and detect fraud and error. Such systems reduce but do not eliminate the risk of mis-statements, and management assumes responsibility for any residual risk.

For many organizations, the responsibility for management to keep proper accounting records and for preparing financial statements giving a true and fair view is set out in relevant legislation (see Chapter 1), such as sections 121 and 123 of the Companies Ordinance in Hong Kong and sections 221 of the Companies Act in the UK. There are other statutory measures relating to management's responsibilities. For instance, consenting to and conniving at false accounting by an organization is an offence under sections 19 and 20 of the Theft Ordinance in Hong Kong and section 17 of the Theft Act in the UK. In addition, the directors of a company have a responsibility to ensure that the company does not engage in fraudulent trading under section 275 of the Companies Ordinance and section 458 of the Companies Act in the UK.

Given the responsibility of directors to prepare financial statements that give a true and fair view of the state of affairs of an organization and of its profit or loss for the financial year, it is necessary, where material error or fraud has occurred, for them to correct the accounting records and ensure that the matter is appropriately reflected and disclosed in the financial statements.[10]

DETERRING, DETECTING AND INVESTIGATING ACCOUNTING IRREGULARITIES

Accounting irregularities may be viewed at three levels – deterrence, detection and investigation. Deterrence involves preventing the accounting irregularities from happening. Detection means how the indication and suspicion of accounting irregularities are identified. Last but not least, once discovered, accounting irregularities are investigated and reported to the relevant authorities.

Prevention is better than cure. The risk of fraud can be reduced through a variety of deterrence measures. Prevention and deterrence measures are much less costly than the time and expense required for detection, investigation and ultimately rectification of the damages resulting from accounting irregularities. Accounting irregularities can be difficult to detect because they often involve concealment through falsification of documents or collusion among management, employees or third parties. Therefore, it is important to place a strong emphasis on deterrents to accounting irregularities. These may reduce opportunities for wrongdoings and malpractices and could dissuade individuals from committing irregularities because of the likelihood of detection and punishment.

We now consider various preventive measures at two different dimensions. Both dimensions are equally important, and balanced attention between the two is needed to maximize the effectiveness of any anti-fraud campaign. Deterrents to accounting irregularities at the micro-level are implemented within the authority of the organization in question. At the macro-level, deterrents to accounting irregularities refer to the external environment and regulatory framework, affecting the aggregate economy as a whole, mostly probably beyond the controls of any organization.

MICRO-DETERRENTS TO ACCOUNTING IRREGULARITIES

There are two main categories of micro-deterrents – internal controls, and people and culture.

INTERNAL CONTROLS

Perpetrators tend to stay away from accounting irregularities unless there is a perceived opportunity of successfully committing and concealing the act. Therefore, at the micro-level, an organization may focus on eliminating or minimizing these perceived opportunities through a three-stage process – gauging the risks, mitigating the risks and implementing effective internal controls.

Gauging the risks of accounting irregularities

The degree of vulnerability of an organization to accounting irregularities depends on a number of factors including the nature and extent of risks and the size and complexity of its operations. However, management should recognize that accounting irregularities can occur in organizations of any size or type, and that almost any employee can become a perpetrator in a certain situation. The risk assessment process should also cover other fraudulent acts, such as misappropriation of assets and corruption.

Mitigating the risks of accounting irregularities

Internal controls are defined as all the policies and procedures adopted by an organization to assist in achieving management's objective of ensuring, as far as practicable, the orderly and efficient conduct of its business, including adherence to management policies, the safeguarding of assets, the prevention and detection of fraud and error, the accuracy and completeness of the accounting records, and the timely preparation of reliable financial information.[11] In addition to those matters directly relating to the accounting system, the internal control system can be viewed in two layers:

- the control environment
- the control procedures.

The control environment refers to the overall attitude, awareness and actions of management regarding the internal control system and its importance in the organization. The control environment may include budgetary controls and internal audit functions and strengthens the effectiveness of specific control procedures. A strong environment can significantly complement specific control procedures, but it does not by itself ensure the effectiveness of the internal control system. Examples of the control environment are as follows:

- the function of the board of directors and its committees;
- management's philosophy and operating style;

- the organization's structure and methods of assigning authority and responsibility;

- management's control system including internal audit function and segregation of duties; and

- management's human resources policies covering recruitment, retention and training aspects.

In addition to the control environment, control procedures refer to those policies and procedures established to achieve the organization's specific objectives. Examples of specific control procedures are as follows:

- reporting, reviewing and approving reconciliations;

- checking the arithmetical accuracy of the records;

- controlling the applications and security of computer information systems and the integrity of the computer data;

- maintaining and reviewing control accounts and trial balances;

- approving and controlling documents;

- comparing internal data with external (and reliable) sources of information;

- carrying out periodic counts on cash and inventories, and comparing the results with records;

- limiting direct physical access to assets and sensitive records;

- comparing and analysing the financial results with budgeted amounts.

In more drastic cases, an organization may minimize (or eliminate completely) certain risks by selling parts of its operations (for example, withdrawal from doing business with certain entities which are deemed to be suspicious and risky); by changing the locations of business (for example, the closure of a branch); or by reorganizing its business processes (for example, a more closely monitored procurement from a pre-approved vendors list).

Implementing effective internal controls

Some risks are inevitable and inherent in the organization's operating environment, but most can be addressed with an appropriate system of internal controls. Once the risks are gauged, the organization can identify the processes and controls to mitigate the identified risks. Deciding what internal controls are effective is a balancing act between costs and benefits. The relevant costs to consider include direct costs of implementing and operating that control as well as indirect costs of having that control in place. Having an internal control in place will often reduce the efficiency of an organization's operations; for example, the organization may take longer to respond to customers because of the reviews and approvals before the transactions are executed.

The main types of internal controls are set out as follows:

- Organizational controls – include a chart of hierarchy defining and assigning authorities, responsibilities and reporting channels covering all aspects of the organization's operations.

- Segregation of duties – refers to the separation of duties such as authorization, execution, custody, recording and system development which would, if combined, enable an individual to record and process a complete transaction.

- Physical controls – refer to the custody of assets and involve security and safeguarding measures designed to ensure that access to assets is limited to authorized personnel.

- Authorization and approval – all transactions require authorization or approval by appropriate responsible persons, possibly with tiers of limits according to the significance and complexity of the transactions.

- Arithmetical and accounting controls – include checking the arithmetical accuracy of the records, the maintenance and checking of totals reconciliations, control accounts and trial balances, and accounting for documents.

- Supervisory and managerial controls – refer to the supervision by responsible officials of day-to-day transactions and the controls exercised by management outside the day-to-day transactions, such as the review of budgets and management accounts and the internal audit function.

In summary, the documents and records of an organization should be arithmetically checked, physically secured, properly reviewed and approved, and confirmed with the relevant external parties, each of which are conducted by different persons. For example, mailing of monthly statements to customers should be done by someone who has no responsibility for handling cash or preparing the sales and account receivable records. Any disagreement with customers should be properly recorded and directed to a responsible person other than the one who handles cash receipts, sales records and account receivable records. Records of disagreements and how they are resolved should be reviewed by senior management.

PEOPLE AND CULTURE

Having the appropriate internal controls in place is a procedure-based type of deterrent. All procedures are implemented by people. The proper functioning of any system depends on the competence and integrity of those operating it. The qualifications, selection and training as well as the personal characteristics of the personnel involved are important features to be considered in setting up any control system.

Accounting irregularities committed by senior management typically involve the override of internal controls within the financial reporting process. Because senior management has the ability to override controls, or to influence others to perpetrate or conceal fraud, the need for a strong culture of good ethics in financial reporting becomes increasingly important. This fosters an environment in which other employees are strong enough to say no to accounting irregularities and to use the appropriate communication channels to report any requests to commit wrongdoing. The potential for senior management override also increases the need for appropriate oversight measures by the board of directors or audit committee, as discussed in the following section.

In addition, the effectiveness of any internal controls is inherently limited by the following factors:[12]

- management's usual requirement that the cost of an internal control does not exceed the expected benefits to be derived;

- most internal controls tend to be directed at routine transactions rather than non-routine transactions;

- the potential for human error due to carelessness, distraction, poor judgement and the misunderstanding of instruction;

- the possibility of by-passing internal controls through the collusion of a member of management or an employee with parties outside or inside the organization;

- the possibility that a person responsible for exercising an internal control could abuse that responsibility;

- the possibility that procedures may become inadequate due to changes in conditions, and compliance with procedures may deteriorate.

Therefore, a culture of good ethics with people of high integrity is necessary to overcome the above weaknesses.

People

Each employee has a unique set of values and personal code of ethics. When faced with sufficient pressure and a perceived opportunity, some employees may be tempted to behave dishonestly. The threshold at which dishonest behaviour starts, however, varies among individuals. If an organization is to be successful in preventing accounting irregularities, it must have effective policies that minimize the chance of hiring or promoting individuals with low levels of honesty, especially for sensitive positions and more senior appointments.

As an effective micro-deterrent against accounting irregularities, recruitment and promotion procedures should include:

- background reference checks on individuals being considered for employment or for promotion to a position of trust;
- initial and continuous training of all employees about the organization's ethical values and code of conduct;
- evaluation of compliance with the ethical values and code of conduct, with violations being addressed immediately.

This training should set clearly the expectations on all employees regarding:

- their duties to communicate certain matters;
- a list of the types of matters, including actual or suspected fraud, to be communicated along with specific examples;
- information on how to communicate those matters.

Poor communication, lack of clear responsibilities, and poor training and promotion opportunities may detract from a positive environment and increase the risk of accounting irregularities. Training should enhance the awareness of possible wrong-doings, which should be pitched in a constructive manner stressing the costs of accounting irregularities and their detrimental effects in other ways on the organization and its employees.

All employees should be required to sign a declaration of compliance in relation to the organization's ethical values and a code of conduct on an annual basis. Requiring periodic affirmation by employees of their responsibilities will not only reinforce the policy but may also deter individuals from wrongdoings and might identify problems before they become significant. Such affirmation may include statements that the individual understands the organization's expectations, has complied with the code of conduct, and is not aware of any violations of the code of conduct other than those listed in the individual's response. Depending on the background and culture, this practice may not be acceptable to some individuals (even though their behaviour may well be perfectly honest). It is vital to make clear this declaration requirement at the time of recruitment. For existing employees, the requirement may be brought in initially on a voluntary basis until they are more familiar with the idea.

Although people with low integrity may just sign a false declaration, most people want to avoid making a false statement in writing. Honest individuals are more likely to return their declarations and to disclose what they know (including any conflicts of interest or other personal exceptions to the code of conduct). Following up suspicious replies or non-replies may uncover significant issues.

Expectations about the consequences of accounting irregularities must be clearly communicated throughout the organization. Making the consequences visible by a pledge to dismiss perpetrators and to refer to the appropriate authorities can be a valuable deterrent to wrongdoing. If wrongdoing occurs and an employee is disciplined, it can be helpful to communicate that fact, on a no-name basis, in an employee newsletter or other regular communication to employees. Seeing that other people are disciplined for wrongdoing increases the perceived likelihood of perpetrators being caught and punished. It also can demonstrate that the organization is committed to an environment of high ethical standards and integrity.

In summary, the way an organization reacts to incidents of alleged or suspected wrongdoings sends a strong deterrent message throughout the organization, helping to reduce the number of future occurrences. The following responsive actions should be taken in dealing with an alleged incidence of fraud:

- A thorough investigation of the incident should be conducted.

- Appropriate and consistent actions should be taken against perpetrators.

- Relevant controls should be assessed and improved.

- Communication and training should occur to reinforce the organization's ethical value, code of conduct and expectations.

Culture

Management should set the right tone at the top for ethical behaviour within the organization. Management cannot act one way and expect others in the organization to behave differently.

Management must show employees through its words and actions that dishonest or unethical behaviour will not be tolerated, even if the result of the action benefits the organization. Double standards must be avoided and all employees should be treated equally, regardless of their position.

An anti-fraud culture is rooted in a strong set of core values that provides the foundation for the development of an ethical framework that deters accounting irregularities, misappropriation of assets, corruption and other illegal acts.

This value system often is reflected in a code of conduct which should underlie the core values of the organization and guide employees in making appropriate decisions during their working day. The code of conduct might include such topics as ethics, confidentiality, conflict of interest, intellectual property, sexual harassment and fraud. The code of conduct should be included in the staff handbook or on the organization's intranet, so it can be referred to when needed.

An anti-fraud charter should be issued by the board of directors, indicating that the fight against fraud and accounting irregularities is endorsed and supported by the senior management of the organization. Employees are less likely to commit fraud and accounting irregularities if they have positive feelings and perceived equality about an organization than when they feel neglected, abused or threatened. The anti-fraud charter should be developed in a participatory and positive manner resulting in employees at all levels taking ownership of its content. The anti-fraud charter should be simple, focused and easily understood, communicated to all employees and drawn to the attention of all contractors and suppliers. The anti-fraud charter should be actively and regularly promoted throughout the organization to all employees, irrespective of grade, position or length of service.

An effective anti-fraud charter should demonstrate the management's determination to:

- take appropriate measures to deter wrongdoing;
- introduce necessary procedures to detect wrongdoing;
- investigate all instances of suspected wrongdoing;
- report all suspected wrongdoing to the appropriate authorities;
- assist the police in the investigation and prosecution of suspected perpetrators;
- recover from perpetrators any assets wrongfully obtained;
- encourage employees to report any suspicion of wrongdoing.

The organization's human resources department often is instrumental in helping to build an ethical culture and workplace environment. Employees should be given the opportunity to provide input to its development and to ensure that the culture and environment remain relevant, clear and fair. Factors that help create an ethical workplace environment and reduce the risk of wrongdoing may include:

- reward systems which are market-orientated, consistent and supportive of the organization's objectives;

- equal employment opportunities;

- team-oriented and participative decision-making policies;

- professionally administered training programmes and a high priority of career development.

Employees should be encouraged and given the means to communicate concerns, anonymously if preferred, about potential violations of the organization's code of conduct, without fear of retaliation. Therefore, another effective micro-deterrent is a whistle-blowing hotline. It is vital to make clear to all employees that whistle-blowing is an essential element in the fight against fraud and accounting irregularities. The reporting mechanism should be clear and visible. The whistle-blowing hotline should be prepared to accept anonymous calls, and the mechanism should be straight-forward and confidential for employees to report a suspected incident. Alternatively, employees are free to report the suspected incidents to their line manager (or to by-pass their immediate line manager if they suspect that the line manager is involved in wrongdoings).

MACRO-DETERRENTS TO ACCOUNTING IRREGULARITIES

At the macro-level, deterrents to accounting irregularities include those measures affecting all individuals and organizations existing in the aggregate economy as a whole. There are two main categories of macro-deterrents – standardization and governance.

STANDARDIZATION

Auditing standards

In Chapter 1, we considered the ambit of GAAP and the financial reporting environment in Hong Kong and the UK. These all serve as a macro-deterrent to accounting irregularities. In addition, there are auditing standards issued by the HKICPA in Hong Kong and the APB in the UK. Every auditor must comply with these auditing standards while performing audits on financial statements. The Companies Ordinance in Hong

Kong and the Companies Act in the UK effectively endorse the legal status of the auditing standards by insisting that only certain eligible members of certain professional bodies may carry out audits for limited companies. Therefore, by imposing more stringent auditing standards, arguably the financial statements would be subject to a more detailed scrutiny. Accordingly, perpetrators would be aware of the increased level of scrutiny resulting in an increased likelihood of their accounting irregularities being detected and accounting irregularities should be deterred. However, all standards and their implementation costs are ultimately borne by consumers, effectively the readers of financial statements.

Globalization of standards

There are differences in international accounting and auditing practices. Globalizing standards across different countries and jurisdictions can reduce the variations which often provide a breeding ground for the perpetrators' creativity.

The comparability of the financial statements in different countries would be improved if similar accounting practices were used, thereby helping readers of financial statements in making decisions relating to overseas organizations. Many organizations are listed on foreign stock exchanges or have operations in foreign countries. These organizations are sometimes required to prepare not only financial statements according to their domestic GAAP but also a set of financial statements for each foreign country in which they operate, prepared in accordance with that country's GAAP. This is costly, inefficient and vulnerable to accounting irregularities. We are witnessing a trend towards a global economy, and the advances in technology make it uncommon for any sizable organizations to operate in isolation from the rest of the world.

However, such globalization is hindered by two factors:

- The nature of economic and political systems – financial reporting is a foundation of capitalist economies, such as the UK, US and Hong Kong. For investors and lenders to have confidence to invest in organizations over which they have limited control, there must be an extensive financial reporting system designed to provide information in a timely, reliable, relevant and comparable manner. In places such as France and Italy which are more accustomed to government intervention and also in certain centrally planned and socialist economies, such as the former Soviet Union or the People's Republic of China, there may be a much greater role for the state in determining accounting requirements, and the accounting requirements may be developed to suit the information needs of the government as much as those of investors and lenders. In addition, in some places, such as Japan, Belgium, Germany and some South American countries, there is a strong association between taxation laws and accounting requirements. Taxation laws are developed to meet specific fiscal goals, such as raising a certain amount of revenue or encouraging a particular economic activity, rather than presenting a true and fair view of an organization's position and performance. Where the accounting requirements are based upon these taxation laws, the resulting financial statements would differ significantly from those which are customary in Hong Kong and the UK.

● The nature of readers – in the UK, US and Hong Kong, the primary readers of financial statements are assumed to be investors and lenders. Consequently, the financial statements provide these readers with the information that they find useful for their investing and lending decisions. In other places, the government may be the primary reader of the financial statements, with the information being used for economic planning and in the determination of taxation liabilities (as in many South American countries). GAAP in such places would be expected to be determined by the information needs of government. In addition, in some places such as the UK, US and Hong Kong, there are mass equity markets, and the existence of many potential investors promotes widespread communications of financial information and supports the development of professional accounting bodies, shareholders' bodies and regulators to protect the interests of this diverse group and ensure that they are provided with the information they need. In other countries such as Japan, Germany and France, there are fewer providers of equity finance and, as a result, there is a concentration of ownership. In some countries, such as Italy, France and Germany, there is also a much greater reliance on debt finance other than equity finance. The owners and debt providers are able to negotiate directly with their borrowers as to the nature, timing and extent of the information that they require. As a consequence, there may be a reduced need for legislative accounting requirements or an organized accounting profession.

GOVERNANCE

More governing regulations on financial reporting, more powers to the regulators and more stringent penalties on non-compliance are all designed to deter perpetrators who would have to think twice before committing any wrongdoings and accounting irregularities.

The term 'corporate governance' refers to the systems and processes adopted to direct and manage the business and operation of a company. Strictly speaking, corporate governance only applies to companies, but non-company entities might adopt it as a voluntary compliance with best practice. Corporate governance is defined by various authorities in different countries, and there are many different groups which have an interest in corporate governance. Different stakeholders' groups focus on different issues and criteria in deciding what comprises good corporate governance from their viewpoint. Shareholders, for example, are most likely to attach the greatest importance to issues and criteria concerned with maximizing the market value of a company's share price on a sustained basis. Regulators are more focused on policy, compliance, supervision and operational issues. Employees look to the company for continued employment opportunities, and other groups have an interest in various social and environmental issues.

Regardless of which definition is preferred, there are two common grounds in corporate governance. Firstly, shareholders have primacy over all other stakeholders' groups as it is their money that is at risk. Secondly, the foundations of corporate governance are based on the way in which organizations are directed and controlled.

In Hong Kong, the HKICPA has published the *Corporate Governance Disclosure in Annual Reports – A Guide to Current Requirements and Recommendations for Enhancement* (the Report) in March 2001. The key recommendations are as follows:

- To communicate to shareholders the strength of their corporate governance structure, policies and practices. Listed companies and public corporations are encouraged to include a statement of corporate governance in their annual report.

- To enhance comparability and transparency of the way directors are compensated, directors' remuneration should be analysed between 'performance based' and 'non-performance based'.

- Disclosure requirements in respect of directors' share options should be extended to include disclosure by individual director of the aggregate value realized. Aggregate value realized is calculated as the excess of the market price on the day of exercise of the option over the exercise price multiplied by the number of shares acquired as a result of the exercise of the options.

- To aid communication with the readers of the financial statements, the directors should set out in a separate statement their responsibilities in connection with the preparation of the financial statements.

- To increase transparency regarding auditors' independence, disclosure of non-audit fees paid to auditors should be made.

In the UK, corporate governance is more sophisticated and its developments started in the late 1980s (following the financial scandals at Maxwell, BCCI and Polly Peck). In 1992, there was the publication of the groundbreaking Cadbury Code of Best Practice (the Cadbury Report). The Cadbury Report has been used as the basis for similar initiatives in other countries and is a primary reason why the UK is regarded as a world leader in the field of corporate governance.

The Cadbury Report has many recommendations including the use of board committees and the separation of the role of Chairman and Chief Executive. One of the recommendations in the Cadbury Report states that boards should report on the effectiveness of systems of internal control. This provision has subsequently been refined in The Rutteman Report (1994) in that those directors should limit their review to internal financial controls and report only that they have carried out a review. Directors should disclose the key procedures that they establish to provide effective internal financial control.

In 1995, following concerns about directors' pay and share options, the Greenbury Report recommended extensive disclosure in annual reports about all the components of, and company policy for determining, directors' remuneration and compensation. The Greenbury Report recommended the establishment of a remuneration committee of the board comprising non-executive directors. Annual reports in the UK now contain extensive information on directors' remuneration and compensation.

In January 1998, the Hampel Report reviewed the Cadbury Report and ensured that its original purpose had been achieved. The Hampel Report:

- keeps under review the role of directors, executive and non-executive;

- follows up relevant matters arising from the Greenbury Report; and

- addresses the role of shareholders and auditors in corporate governance issues.

In June 1998, following the publication of the Hampel report, the UK Listing Authority published the Combined Code. Appended to the listing rules, the Combined Code states that corporate governance principles should be applied flexibly, with common sense, having regard to a company's individual circumstances. Companies must explain in their annual report how they have applied the 14 principles and the extent of their compliance with the 45 provisions, or give reasons for their non-compliance. Disclosures are therefore essential. The company's external auditors are required to review the directors' compliance statements for 7 of the 45 provisions. One of the principles and its related two provisions relate to the board's maintenance of a sound system of internal control. This covers the wider aspects of internal control (that is, not limited to internal financial control) and one of the two provisions makes reference to risk management.

The Institute of Chartered Accountants in England & Wales (ICAEW) provides guidance on internal control as to how the relevant provision in the Combined Code should be applied. In September 1999, the ICAEW published the Turnbull Report. The Turnbull Report relates internal control to the management of risk to a company's objectives, and recommends a risk-based approach to establishing a sound system of internal control and reviewing its effectiveness. In addition to establishing and maintaining relevant policies and procedures to implement the report recommendations, directors should state in their annual report that there is an ongoing process for identifying, evaluating and managing the significant risks faced by the company.

From a brief analysis of the many international and national codes of good corporate governance, it is possible to summarize the guiding principles and best practices as follows:

- Governance structures need to be designed with clear delineation of power, responsibilities, checks and balances including the establishment of board committees (such as the audit committee) to look at complex and detailed areas.

- Accountability and control are fundamental but they can only be safeguarded if sufficient disclosure and transparency are guaranteed when reporting to the market.

- The members of the board must be selected according to the principles of professionalism and ethical behaviour. Non-executive directors should also be independent.

- There should be formal and transparent arrangements for maintaining an appropriate relationship with the company's auditors, which is usually the responsibility of the audit committee.

Let us briefly consider three key components of good corporate governance as a deterrent to accounting irregularities – the audit committee, non-executive directors and the management of risk.

Audit committees

The Combined Code requires companies listed on the London Stock Exchange to have an audit committee entirely composed of non-executive directors (NEDs). Audit committees give additional assurance to shareholders about the quality and reliability of the financial statements issued by a company. They also deal with matters relating to the internal and external auditors.

Auditing standards in the UK require the external auditor of a listed company to provide the audit committee with a written statement, at least annually, about the audit firm's independence and in particular the objectivity of the audit engagement partner and audit staff. Where an audit committee operates effectively, it has the potential to:

- improve the quality of financial reporting and thereby increase public confidence in the credibility and objectivity of financial statements;

- enable the NEDs to contribute an independent judgement in running the business;

- assist the finance director to raise issues of concern;

- strengthen the positions of the external and internal auditors by allowing them to raise issues of concern direct to the audit committee.

There are other issues that the board can ask the audit committee to deal with, such as:

- asking challenging questions about the processes related to identification, management and monitoring of the significant risks facing the company and the related internal control issues;

- being the focal point for internal reporting on matters such as whistle-blowing;

- focusing attention on the need for proper policies and procedures to help prevent fraud and irregularities;

- acting as the lead committee on matters related to compliance with corporate governance practices.

Having independent NEDs on the audit committee is therefore essential, but it is not enough by itself. If they are to make an effective contribution to the work of the committee, these individuals need to ask perceptive and challenging questions of management and the executive directors.

It also needs to be emphasized that, by itself, even an effective audit committee is not guaranteed to prevent accounting irregularities but it can play a valuable part in reducing such dangers. Other parties have their role to play, not least of which is the board of directors itself.

Non-executive directors

In addition to the audit committee, the NEDs sit on two other important committees of the board: the remuneration committee and the nomination committee. The remuneration committee reviews and recommends the remuneration package of each director for the board's approval. The nomination committee seeks and nominates appropriate individuals for directorship for the board's approval. The NEDs' independent input is fundamental to these committees, as well as to the board itself, but their role is not easy in today's complex business environment.

There are various considerations to make in this respect, such as:

- how to define the population of NEDs (who are they, how are they appointed, how the pool might be widened);

- how to assess their independence and effectiveness;

- how to determine their accountability (their relationships with institutional investors);

- how to deal with issues relating to NEDs' remuneration;

- how to ensure NEDs obtain a good understanding of the business of a company;

- how to address the liability issue which would otherwise deter good candidates from serving as NEDs.

Management of risks

A common factor in some of the recent corporate collapses has been the lack of effective systems of internal control and risk management. The Turnbull Report recommends a risk-based approach in establishing a sound, broadly based system of internal control with board review of its effectiveness. The Turnbull Report, which is based on a framework approach, proposed that to reflect sound business practice, internal control should:

- be embedded in a company's processes;

- remain relevant over time in the continually evolving business environment;

- form part of the corporate culture.

The Turnbull Report sets out the duties of boards of directors in relation to internal control and the management of risk, and notes that their ultimate responsibilities cannot be delegated. The Turnbull Report also states that all employees have some responsibilities for internal control and should collectively have the necessary knowledge, skills, information and authority to establish, operate and monitor the necessary systems.

The Turnbull Report recommends that to ensure that they remain effective, systems of internal control and risk management must be subjected to ongoing monitoring through regular reviews by management and internal audit. The board should regularly receive and review reports on internal control, undertake its own annual assessment and state in the annual report that:

- there is an ongoing process for identifying, evaluating and managing significant risks faced by the company;

- it has been in place for the year up to the date of the approval of the annual report and accounts;

- it is regularly reviewed by the board;

- it accords with the guidance in the Turnbull Report.

Although the recommendations of the Turnbull report were seen as stringent, it has been generally well received in the United Kingdom and is respected overseas.

The importance of corporate governance is growing because it is concerned with both the effectiveness and the accountability of boards of directors. The effectiveness of boards, which covers the quality of leadership and direction they provide, can be measured over time by performance in earnings and the share price. Accountability, which is key to corporate governance, will include the issues surrounding disclosure and transparency of communications to shareholders.

CONCLUSION

Fraud ranges from petty theft and unproductive behaviour to accounting irregularities and misappropriation of assets. Accounting irregularities have a significant adverse effect on an organization's market value, reputation and ability to accomplish its strategic mission. Highly publicized cases raise the awareness of the effects of accounting irregularities and lead many organizations to be more proactive in taking steps to deter their occurrence. Misappropriation of assets that are not necessarily material to the financial statements can nonetheless result in substantial losses to an organization.

The degree to which certain specific programmes and general internal controls are applied in smaller, less complex organizations are likely to differ from larger organizations. Implementing a system of internal controls can only be conducted in accordance with the nature and size of the organization, but some smaller organizations may find that certain types of control activities are not relevant because of the close involvement and control by the owners in the management of the organization.

Effective deterrents to accounting irregularities require changes in procedures, regulations as well as behaviour. Ultimately, the real deterrents can only materialize with social changes, which in turn can only be cultivated through continuous knowledge, market incentives and a genuine willingness to change. Organizations and society at large must make it clear that unethical or dishonest behaviour is unacceptable.

Narrowing the differences amongst different jurisdictions and globalizing the standards can eliminate the degree of undue variations in financial reporting. Corporate governance, comprising increasing transparency in financial reporting and the new concepts of audit committees, NEDs and management of risks, can certainly be a major deterrent against accounting irregularities.

Notes

1, 3, 8, 9, 10 – SAS 110 *Fraud and Error* (issued by the APB in January 1995, effective for accounting periods ending on or after 30 June 1995)

1, 2, 3, 4, 5, 6, 7, 8, 9 – SAS 110 *The Auditors' Responsibility to Consider Fraud and Error in an Audit of Financial Statements* (issued by the HKICPA in February 2002, effective for accounting periods ending on or after 31 March 2002)

11, 12 – SAS 300 *Audit Risk Assessments and Accounting and Internal Control Systems* (issued by the HKICPA in January 1997, revised January 2004, effective for accounting periods starting on or before 15 December 2004)

11, 12 – SAS 300 *Accounting and Internal Control Systems and Audit Risk Assessments* (issued by the APB in March 1995, effective for accounting periods ending on or after 23 December 1995)

Glossary

Account	A way of categorizing similar transactions and gathering all financial transactions and activities of an organization affecting a particular reported item in its *financial statements*.
Accounting	An information-processing subject applying to the classification and recording of monetary transactions, and the presentation of the financial results of an organization.
Accounting equation	Forming the foundation of *double-entry* which means that an organization's assets less its *liabilities* should always equal to its *capital*.
Accounting irregularity	Intentional mis-statements or omissions of amounts or disclosures in financial statements.
Accounting policy	Principles, bases, conventions, rules and practices adopted by an organization in preparing and presenting *financial statements*.
Accruals	One of the fundamental concepts in financial reporting, assuming that revenue and costs are recognized as they are earned or incurred, regardless of when the cash is received or paid.
Amortization	Referring to the *depreciation* on intangible assets.
ASB	Accounting Standards Board which develops, issues and withdraws accounting standards (*FRS*s) in the UK.
Assets	An *organization's* rights to receive some economic benefits as a result of past transactions or events.
Audit committee	A committee appointed by the board of directors in charge of various matters in relation to the

organization's (corporation's) audit and *financial statements.*

Auditing

The process of examining and testing the accounts of an organization and their supporting documents in order to express an opinion as to the truth and fairness of the *financial statements.*

Audit trail

The linkage between source documents and figures on *financial statements.*

Average cost method

The average (or weighted average) of the cost of similar items at the beginning of a financial year and the cost of similar items purchased or produced during the financial year.

Balance sheet

One key component of the *financial statements*, the first part of which lists the fixed and current *assets* less the *liabilities*, and the second part of which shows how they have been financed through *capital* (also see *financial statements*).

Below-the-line

A term referring to that part of the *profit and loss account* below the measurement of earnings capacity.

'Big-bath'

A *write-off* or provision making the balance sheet overly conservative and creating a higher degree of manoeuvre for profits (by having fewer expenses in future years' *profit and loss account*).

'Bill and hold' sales

Recorded sales as requested and accepted by customers before the delivery of goods or services.

Break-up value

The aggregate market value of an organization as if each of its parts operated independently and had its own individual price.

Business combination

The combination of two or more *organizations* into a single economic entity under a common management.

Business valuation, asset-based
Valuation of a business on the basis of the worth of its net assets rather than its earning capacity (also see *business valuation, earning-based*).

Business valuation, earning-based
Valuation of a business on the basis of its earning capacity rather than the worth of its net assets (also see *business valuation, asset-based*).

Capital
Owners' equity which represents the owners' investment into the *organization* plus its accumulated net profits (capital is equal to *assets* less *liabilities*).

Capitalization
Reporting an expense as part of the cost of an *asset*.

Cash flow statement
Listing the actual cash received and paid out of an *organization* over a specific period of time (also see *financial statements*).

Comparability
One of the qualitative characteristics of financial information assuming that comparable information refers to *consistency* in each financial year and from one financial year to the next.

Consistency
One of the fundamental concepts in financial reporting, treating like items within each financial year and from one year to the next in a consistent manner (refer to *comparability*).

Consolidation
The process of adjusting and combining financial information from the individual *financial statements* of a *parent* company and its *subsidiaries* to prepare consolidated *financial statements*, such that these consolidated statements present financial information for the group as a single economic entity.

Constructive obligation
An obligation (or a valid expectation on an organization) deriving from the *organization*'s actions which have indicated to other parties that it will accept certain responsibilities through its own announcements, established practices and published policies.

Contingent asset

A possible asset that arises from past events and whose existence will be confirmed only by the occurrence or non-occurrence of one or more uncertain future events not wholly within the control of the *organization*.

Contingent liability

A possible obligation that arises from past events and whose existence will be confirmed only by the occurrence or non-occurrence of one or more uncertain future events not wholly within the control of the organization (alternatively, a present obligation that arises from past events but is not recognized).

'Cookie-jar'

Similar to *big-bath*, an accrual of expenses making the balance sheet overly conservative and creating an undue high degree of flexibility for profits (by having fewer expenses in future years' *profit and loss accounts*).

Corporate governance

The systems and processes adopted by an *organization* (corporation) to direct and manage its business and operation.

Creative accounting

Accounting that takes advantage of the built-in flexibility of the *GAAP* with a dishonest intent and presents a distorted financial picture of an *organization* (also regarded as the first tier of *accounting irregularities*).

Creditor

One to whom money is owed (also known as *accounts payable*).

Debtor

One who owes money to another (also known as *accounts receivable*).

Debtor turnover days

The average number of days that a debtor takes to settle the account balance (it is equal to the average debtor balance, multiplied by 365 days and divided by the credit sales).

Depreciation

A measure of wearing out of a tangible *asset* that is calculated annually and charged as an *expense* in the *profit and loss account*.

Double-entry	A method of recording transactions of an *organization* in a set of accounts, such that every transaction has a dual aspect and therefore needs to be recorded in at least two accounts.
Expense	The outflow of *assets* or the creation of *liabilities* in an effort to generate *revenues* for an *organization*.
FIFO	First-in-first-out assuming that the items of inventory which were purchased or produced first are sold first; and that the items remaining in inventory at the financial year-end are those recently purchased or produced.
Financial reporting	A term referring to *financial statements* and how they are reported.
Financial reporting environment	The environment in which organizations' financial statements are reported (it is a high-level umbrella term covering *GAAP*, the frequency and distribution of *financial statments*, and the composition and function of board of directors).
Financial statements	Mainly including *profit and loss accounts, balance sheets, cash flow statements* and *notes to the financial statements.*
Financial year	A unit of time, usually 12 months, for which *revenues* and *expenses* are recorded and reported (also known as accounting period).
Fixed assets	The *assets*, such as buildings and machinery, that are bought for long-term use in an *organization* rather than for resale (also known as non-current assets).
Forensic accountants	A term referring to practising accountants in the role of investigator and/or expert witness offering quantifiable accounting, auditing and business advice to make the most of the financial aspects in the areas of litigation, dispute resolution and fraud investigation.

Fraud   A deliberate deception in order to obtain unfair and
                                  unlawful gains including *accounting irregularities*.

FRS   Financial Reporting Standards which are issued by the
                                  ASB to gradually replace *SSAPs* in the UK.

GAAP   Generally accepted accounting principles which
                                  represent rules from all authoritative sources
                                  governing accounting.

Gearing   A term referring to the debt to equity ratio of an
                                  organization.

General ledger   Accounting record containing accounts for each *asset*,
                                  liability, *capital*, *revenue* and *expense* (also known as
                                  nominal ledger).

Going concern   One of the fundamental concepts in financial
                                  reporting assuming that the *organization* will continue
                                  in operational existence for the foreseeable future.

Goodwill   The excess of the cost of an acquisition over the fair
                                  value of the acquirer's share of the net *assets* of the
                                  acquiree at the date of acquisition (may be interpreted
                                  as the value of a well-respected business name, good
                                  customer relations or high employee morale).

HKAS   Hong Kong Accounting Standards which are to replace
                                  the *SSAP* and are themselves to be phased out gradually
                                  and replaced by the *HKFRS* in order to harmonize the
                                  accounting standards in Hong Kong with the *IFRS*.

HKFRS   Hong Kong Financial Reporting Standards which set
                                  out recognition, measurement, presentation and
                                  disclosure requirements dealing with transactions
                                  and events and are to replace the *HKAS*.

HKICPA   Hong Kong Institute of Certified Public Accountants
                                  which is the only statutory body to license and
                                  regulate professional accountants in Hong Kong.
                                  Formerly known as the Hong Kong Society of
                                  Accountants, until 2004.

IAS	International Accounting Standards which are issued by the *IASC* and are being phased out by the *IFRS*.
IASB	International Accounting Standards Board which assumed accounting standard-setting responsibilities in 2001 from its predecessor body, the *IASC*.
IASC	International Accounting Standards Committee which was formed in 1973 and was replaced by the *IASB* in 2001.
IFRS	International Financial Reporting Standards which are issued by the *IASB* to replace the *IAS*.
Internal control	Policies and procedures which provide reasonable assurance those specific objectives of the *organization* will be achieved.
Inventories	Raw materials, work-in-progress and finished goods held by an *organization* for production or resale purposes.
Liabilities	An *organization*'s obligations to transfer some economic benefits as a result of past transactions or events.
LIFO	Last-in-first-out assuming that the items of inventory which were purchased or produced last are sold first; and that the items remaining in inventory at the financial year-end are those first purchased or produced.
Liquidity	The speed with which an *asset* can be converted into cash (also see *solvency*).
Materiality	One of the fundamental concepts in financial reporting assuming that material information enhances the usefulness of the *financial statements* in the eyes of the *readers*.
Minority interest	That part of the net results of operations and of net *assets* of a *subsidiary* attributable to interests which

are not owned, directly or indirectly through *subsidiaries*, by the *parent company*.

NBV   Net book value referring to the monetary value assigned to an item on the *balance sheet*.

Notes to financial statements Narrative notes with certain figures as required by the respective *GAAP*, such as principal accounting policies and directors' remuneration (also see *financial statements*).

NRV   Net realizable value referring to the net cash amount expected from the sale of an item, usually equal to the selling price of the item less the cost to complete and sell it.

Off-balance-sheet financing A way of raising finance without reflecting those borrowings in an *organization*'s *balance sheet* as *liabilities*.

Off-book frauds   Frauds or accounting irregularities which are never recorded on the accounting records.

Offsetting   One of the fundamental concepts in financial reporting assuming that *assets, liabilities, capital, revenues* and *expenses* should not be offset unless the offsetting is required by the *GAAP*.

Organizations   Referring to companies, partnerships, trusts, charities, sole proprietorships or other forms of entities requiring the preparation of *financial statements*.

Parent   Parent (or parent company) referring to an *organization* with the controlling interests in its *subsidiaries* (*consolidated financial statements* of the parent include the *financial statements* of all *subsidiaries* under its control).

Perpetrator   A person who plots or commits accounting *irregularities*.

Phantom sales   Recorded sales which are fictitious and for non-existent goods or services.

Probable
(In the context of the *GAAP*) being more likely than not that an event is to occur causing a transfer of economic benefits.

Profit and loss account
One key component of the *financial statements* setting out an *organization*'s total *revenues* and *expenses* within a financial year (also see *financial statements*).

Provision for doubtful debts
A charge in the *profit and loss account* for those debts that might go bad (remain unpaid) in the future.

Prudence
One of the fundamental concepts in financial reporting assuming that revenue and profits are not anticipated, but are recognized in the *profit and loss account* only when realized in the form either of cash or of *assets*, the ultimate cash realization of which can be assessed with reasonable certainty.

Quasi-subsidiary
A vehicle which does not fulfil the definition of a *subsidiary* but gives rise to benefits that in substance are no different from those that would arise were the vehicle a *subsidiary*.

Readers
Readers of *financial statements* or users of the information in the *financial statements* in making their economic decisions.

Relevance
One of the qualitative characteristics of financial information assuming that relevant information has the ability to influence the *readers*' economic decisions.

Related party
Those parties with who the *organization* has a relationship which might destroy the self-interest of one of the parties because accounting is based on measurement of arm's-length transactions.

Reliability
One of the qualitative characteristics of financial information assuming that reliable information reflects the substance of the underlying events and transactions.

Revenue	The inflow or other enhancements of *assets* of an *organization* or settlement of its *liabilities* (or a combination of both).
Revocable sales	Recorded sales which are provisional and incomplete, and can be revoked.
Segregation of duties	Assigning different people the responsibilities of authorizing transactions, recording transactions and maintaining custody of *assets*.
Side letter	A term referring to an attachment or supplementary clauses to a master agreement.
Solvency	An *organization*'s ability to meet debts as they come due (also see *liquidity*).
SSAP	Statements of Standard Accounting Practices which used to be the dominant part of the accounting standards in Hong Kong and the UK (SSAP are now being phased out by *HKAS* and *FRS*).
Stewardship	Meaning that stewards have to account to the owners for their stewardship of the owners' money, and that, in the modern world, accounting is used to keep track of what has been done with the financial resources entrusted to its stewards – the managers or directors.
Subsidiary	An *organization* which is controlled by another entity, called the *parent* (or holding company).
Substance over form	One of the concepts in financial reporting where real commercial substance takes precedence over legal form.
Tax evasion	Any efforts by taxpayers to evade tax by various illegal means, such as not declaring all their income to the tax authorities or falsely claiming relief to which they are not entitled.
Trial balance	A three-column list of account titles and their balances (either debit or credit) per the *general ledger*, as at the financial year-end date.

True and fair view   The overriding legal requirement for financial
                                  reporting in Hong Kong and the UK but is undefined
                                  by law (in essence, it is up to the professional
                                  accountants sector to define its meaning through
                                  compliance with the *GAAP*).

Understandability   One of the qualitative characteristics of financial
                                  information assuming that understandable
                                  information is capable of being understood by *readers*
                                  with a reasonable knowledge of business and
                                  accounting.

Write-off   Charging an *asset* amount to *expense* or loss with an
                                  effect of reducing the value of the *asset*.

Index

About the Author

BENNY K. B. KWOK

郭 啟 彬

BSc CFE DipBA FCA FCPA FTIHK MBA MCIJ
www.BennyKwok.com

Benny K. B. Kwok is an acknowledged expert in the fields of litigation support, dispute analysis and fraud investigation, practising in the UK and Hong Kong. He is the author of another authoritative title *Forensic Accountancy*. During the 1980–90s, Mr Kwok worked for KPMG, PwC, Abbey National Bank and the Audit Commission in the UK.

Having founded the forensic department for a major firm in 2001, Benny K. B. Kwok now runs an independent accounting practice in Hong Kong. He holds a number of public appointments in Hong Kong, including the Adjudicator to the Obscene Articles Tribunal (the Obscene and Indecent Articles Ordinance) and Member of the Board of Review (the Inland Revenue Ordinance), and sits on six committees of the Hong Kong Institute of Certified Public Accountants including the Investigation Committee, the Complaint Committee and the Expert Panel on Legal Matters. Benny K. B. Kwok is a Certified Fraud Examiner and serves as the Honorary Treasurer in its Hong Kong Chapter.

A sought-after speaker, he has delivered more than 50 courses and seminars for the Hong Kong Government and a number of institutions. To demonstrate a multiple of talents, Benny K. B. Kwok is a Fellow of the Taxation Institute of Hong Kong and a qualified journalist with the Chartered Institute of Journalists in the UK. He has had more than 100 articles published in a wide range of journals and daily newspapers, including the Institute of Chartered Accountants in England & Wales, the CPA Australia, the Canadian Association of Certified General Accountants, the Chinese Institute of Certified Public Accountants, the Hong Kong Institute of Certified Public Accountants, the Law Society of Hong Kong, the Hong Kong Institute of Company Secretaries, the Hong Kong Institute of Bankers, the Hong Kong Institute of Human Resources Management and the Hong Kong Confederation of Insurance Brokers.